The Art of Investing and Portfolio Management

A Proven 6-Step Process to Meet Your Financial Goals

Ronald Cordes

Brian O'Toole

Richard Steiny

McGraw-Hill

New York   Chicago   San Francisco   Lisbon   London   Madrid
Mexico City   Milan   New Delhi   San Juan   Seoul
Singapore   Sydney   Toronto

The McGraw·Hill Companies

1 2 3 4 5 6 7 8 9 0 DOC/DOC 0 9 8 7 6 5 4

ISBN 0-07-144005-4

This publication is designed to provide accurate and authoritative information in regard to the subject matter covered. It is sold with the understanding that neither the author nor the publisher is engaged in rendering legal, accounting, or other professional service. If legal advice or other expert assistance is required, the services of a competent professional person should be sought.

> —*From a declaration of Principles jointly adopted by a Committee of the American Bar Association and a Committee of Publishers.*

McGraw-Hill books are available at special quantity discounts to use as premiums and sales promotions, or for use in corporate training programs. For more information, please write to the Director of Special Sales, McGraw-Hill Professional, Two Penn Plaza, New York, NY 10011-2298. Or contact your local bookstore.

The CFP® certification mark is owned by the Certified Financial Planner Board of Standards, Inc.

 This book is printed on recycled, acid-free paper containing a minimum of 50% recycled de-inked fiber.

Library of Congress Cataloging-in-Publication Data

Cordes, Ron, 1959-
    The art of investing and strategic portfolio management :
    a proven 6-step process to meet your financial goals / By
    Ron Cordes, Brian O'Toole, and Richard Steiny.
        p.   cm.
    ISBN 0-07-144005-4 (cloth : alk. paper)
    1. Finance, Personal.   2. Investments.   3. Portfolio
    management.   I. O'Toole, Brian, 1958-   II. Steiny, Richard.
    III. Title.
    HG179.C682 2004   2004
    332.024—dc22   2003024379

To our retired partner, Richard T. O'Toole, whose guidance and vision over two decades inspired the growth and success of our organization.

Contents

Preface

*W*hen we first sat down to start writing this book, the date was March 10th, 2003—exactly three years to the day that the Nasdaq Composite Index closed at its all time high of 5048. It's safe to say that few investors, ourselves included, woke up that Friday in 2000 thinking that the end of the longest bull market in history was upon us. But just a few weeks later, the Standard & Poor's 500 and the Dow Jones Industrial Average reached their peaks and the market began a truly dizzying downward spiral. The party was officially over.

By the end of 2002, stocks had posted three consecutive years of losses—a feat that previously had occurred just three times since 1900. The Standard & Poor's 500 was down 42 percent from its high, while the Nasdaq had plummeted 74 percent. Meanwhile, a staggering $7 trillion of investors' wealth was erased from late March 2000 through early October 2002.

The severity of the market downturn meant that few investors—even those with significant wealth and experience—were left unscathed. Consider your own portfolio's performance during this incredibly volatile period: Did you watch much of your hard-earned wealth vanish? If so, you've got plenty of company. A Merrill Lynch study conducted in 2002 revealed that a stunning 97.4 percent of affluent Americans with investable assets of between $100,000 and $1 million lost money in their investment accounts from the market peak in early 2000 to December 2002. More than one-third (34.7 percent) lost 51 percent or more.

Then, in 2003, the stock market finally regained some of its strength: The Standard & Poor's 500 rose 26 percent while the Nasdaq soared 50 percent.

So where does that leave us now, after three years of dreadful returns and one year of strong gains? If you're like most investors, confusion, uncertainty, fear and frustration dominate your thoughts. You hope, of course, that the market's impressive performance of late will continue—but you remain worried that yet another blow-up may be right around the corner. You know that you must invest wisely in order to achieve the financial goals you desire for yourself and your family. But after being so badly burned—perhaps by your own lack of investing acumen, by following hot tips or media hype, or even by a stockbroker or other financial "expert" who didn't have your best interests at heart—you're unsure of what to do next. "There must be a better way to invest," you lament. "If only I could find it."

You're the reason why we've written this book. We felt a great deal of frustration watching investors in recent years follow the generally poor advice offered up by some members of the investment community, the media and the throngs of self-proclaimed investment gurus. We've learned through our extensive experience that there is an approach to investing that is fundamentally different and superior—and we want to share that approach with you so that you can achieve consistent investment success.

The three of us have worked together for more than twenty years to help investors manage their money, both as financial advisors and now as partners in a successful money management firm that brings world-class investment solutions to advisors and their clients. Our mission has always been to give investors the framework they need to make smart decisions, invest more confidently, focus on what's truly important while tuning out the noise, and realize their financial dreams. We emphatically believe that investors owe it to themselves and their families to use the processes and capabilities that give them the best chance of reaching their most important financial goals. And we believe that it's our job to provide investors with these crucial processes and capabilities.

A Better Path to Investment Success

*I*f you're among the millions of investors who have suffered losses during the past several years—or if you feel at all uncertain about how to manage your investment assets—one lesson is clear: You need a better way to invest. That is exactly what we will give you. By following the advice in this book, you will take your investing to the next level and achieve a degree of success that you may not have thought possible.

To truly become the most successful investor you can be, you must understand and consistently implement the very best strategies of the top investment minds. This is what this book will teach you. You will learn how the world's premier investors—a select group of large institutional investment firms—manage money for their clients so that you can emulate their approach when it comes to building and maintaining your own investment portfolio.

Traditionally, investors have had no way to access these institutional strategies, which have been reserved for huge pension plans, endowments, trusts, charitable organizations, and the like. We will open the door to those strategies, and you will see that they offer a consistent, time-tested approach to managing your money—one that has the disciplined processes and unsurpassed capabilities in place to maximize your chances of achieving true investment success.

Most investors as well as investment advisors do not manage money the way this elite group of financial institutions does. The biggest problem is that they lack a disciplined approach that keeps them on track. Instead, they get caught up in their own emotional responses to market fluctuations. Rational thought flies out the window as emotions become the primary driver of investment decisions.

Think about your own investment history. Have you consistently made investment decisions based on a disciplined, rational process that takes all the facts into account? Or have enthusiasm, greed, fear, and panic caused you to buy and sell investments at the wrong times?

As you'll see early in this book, breaking the cycle of emotion-based investing is difficult—but you can do it. Our proven six-step investment process will help to keep you from getting caught up in the emotions that accompany market extremes and that are fueled every day by the media. By implementing this process, you will no longer be swayed by those feelings. You will no longer be a victim to hype. Instead, you will have put in place a proven system for building and maintaining an investment plan that will work for you regardless of the market environment. By the time you finish reading this book, you will feel empowered to consistently make smarter, more successful investment decisions—and stick to them through thick and thin.

"I'VE HEARD THIS ALL BEFORE"

If your first reaction to our proposition is skepticism, we don't blame you. The excesses of the bull market, as well as the frustrations of the bear market, are almost too numerous to count, and they've left investors feeling justifiably suspicious. In much the same way that investors during the late 1990s expected the good times to roll on forever, many in 2003 predicted that the bad times would continue indefinitely—and they avoided stocks like the plague. "Why not give up?" said these jaded investors. "The can't-fail strategies we used back in the late 1990s blew up in our faces! We're not putting our faith in any more advice from these so-called professionals."

Compounding this doubt is the fact that the sheer amount of financial advice available to investors has become overwhelming. Insurance agents, certified public accountants (CPAs), and other types of professionals are all working harder than ever to provide a broad range of financial solutions. This has made it an especially tough job to wade through all the options that exist and find advice you can truly trust.

We think a good dose of skepticism is healthy. A skeptical investor realizes that investing is difficult and requires hard work and that there are no gimmicks, tricks, or magic beans that can generate long-term success.

We couldn't agree more. Managing money is an extremely difficult job. It's tough for the biggest investment firms in the world that devote themselves entirely to the task, let alone for the average person trying to juggle the demands of daily life. As we've always preached to our clients, you cannot achieve consistent success by treating investing as a hobby or sport. Sure, it might be fun to occasionally get some "down home" advice offered by amateur investors such as the Beardstown Ladies Investment Club. The problem is, those investors simply do not have the experience, disciplined processes, and world-class capabilities that we emphatically believe are necessary to achieve success.

As you'll discover, our process flies in the face of the hot tips and strategies-du-jour offered by the financial press (whose true job is to sell advertising, not provide quality advice), the investment gurus, the "talking heads" on CNBC, and the vast majority of financial advisors and stockbrokers you'll encounter. Once you see how compelling our six-step process is, you'll find it easy to tune out all that noise. The only reason you'll pick up the latest magazine proclaiming, "The Seven Stocks to Own—Now!" is because you need a good laugh.

Still, we invite you to keep your "skeptic's hat" on for the time being. We are certain that the evidence we present in this book will convince you overwhelmingly to adopt an institutional-class investment approach. The reason for our confidence is simple: We have used this approach ourselves for more than 10 years to achieve success for thousands of investors like yourself. Our process is built on world-renowned investment theories and has been used successfully in the real world time and time again to help investors just like you achieve their most important financial goals.

OUR STORY

We once felt about investing the same way that many of you are feeling today. During the 1980s, we ran a financial planning firm in the San Francisco area, working directly with hundreds of individual investors. Although achieving our clients' goals was always our top priority, we found that our investment results often fell short of our expectations. Despite our best intentions, we weren't serving our clients as well as they deserved. This obviously frustrated us but also strengthened our resolve to find a solution that would deliver the results we sought.

Therefore, we carefully examined how we did our job as advisors in order to identify areas of improvement. We looked at our investment processes, as well as at the investing habits of our clients and other investors, and we learned several important lessons that fundamentally altered our viewpoint both as investors and as financial advisors.

- *Emotions drive us to make mistakes.* As you'll see in Chapter 2, emotions constantly get the best of investors. When stock prices soar for extended periods, for example, caution gives way to overconfidence and greed. When stocks plummet, we experience denial, concern, and eventually fear and despair. These emotional reactions cause us to make irrational and costly mistakes: chasing after last year's hottest asset class, buying overpriced assets while ignoring underpriced investments, turning over our holdings excessively, and/or buying a fund based entirely on its five-star rating—the list of bad behavior goes on and on.

- *Information alone doesn't cut it.* As financial advisors, we were able to get our hands on huge amounts of data and the latest technology. Yet our portfolios often delivered subpar performance. The lesson we learned is that information and good intentions are not enough by themselves to generate consistent investment success. Investors also must arm themselves with the right capabilities. In our experience, we had to admit that we alone didn't have the capabilities to transform all our information consistently into knowledge that we could use to build superior portfolios.

This problem is significantly more pervasive today. Think about it: You're bombarded with information from the Internet, financial television channels, magazines, friends, and family—perhaps even your golf partners. This avalanche of information is simply too much for most of us to take in and process in a way that allows us to make truly smart, useful investment decisions. Instead of using all this information intelligently, we become bogged down in it. The result: We forget about risk and volatility and chase after the asset classes that have posted the hottest performance over 1 week, 1 month or 1 quarter—only to get burned down the road.

As these valuable lessons began to sink in, our next step became clear. We needed to find an investment approach that eliminated emotion from the decision-making process. This approach also had to provide us with tremendous capabilities that would help us to make smarter decisions for our clients.

After several months of research and evaluation, we found the solution among an elite group of the nation's top institutional investment firms, such as Goldman Sachs, Standard & Poor's, UBS Global Asset Management, and Wilshire Associates. As we met with members of these firms and analyzed their processes, we were extremely impressed with what we discovered—a foundation in cutting-edge, unbiased academic investment research; disciplined investment processes built around fundamentals, not emotion; investment policy committees made up of professionals with decades of investment experience; teams of portfolio strategists that placed enormous emphasis on the process of asset allocation (how money is divided among stocks, bonds, and other types of assets); and rigorous evaluation processes for selecting and monitoring money managers.

In short, these firms operated with a level of discipline and sophistication unlike anything we'd seen. They assigned crucial investment decisions to experienced strategists—who evaluated historical rates of return, risk management, and other issues instead of relying on short-term performance or chasing "hot" stocks or funds. These strategists, in turn, were supported by huge teams of experienced professionals around the globe. A close look at these firms' performance reports proved what we suspected: They had been able consistently to deliver the best possible returns for a given level of risk.

We knew we had found an approach that worked. Unfortunately, these remarkable strategies and capabilities were, at the time, available only to large institutions and the very wealthiest private investors. Our job became to change all that by providing investors with the same high-quality resources that such companies and institutions as Carnegie Mellon University, Eastman Kodak, the Commonwealth of Massachusetts, Shell Oil, Sony Corporation, and the World Bank have at their disposal.[1] We believed emphatically then as we do today that individual investors deserve nothing less than the same level of expertise that these organizations enjoy.

AN OVERVIEW OF OUR INSTITUTIONAL APPROACH

Our investment process is rooted in the disciplined approach and world-class capabilities that these institutions offer their clients. As you read on, you may be surprised by the nature of our process. It's not aimed at showing you how to time the markets, and we won't attempt to show you how to bet on short-term themes that lead to the "easy money." Those and similar flashy strategies treat investing as sport and aren't worth the paper they're printed on.

What we will promise to do is to share with you a process that will refocus the energy you exert on investing away from those distractions. It will build in a discipline that will keep you from being caught up in the media noise and the emotions of a very exciting marketplace or a very depressing marketplace, as well as stop you from making extreme decisions at extreme times in the market.

Our 6-step process is guided by seven key principles, which we'll detail in the coming chapters.

1. *Emphasize a disciplined process to eliminate an emotional response to short-term market volatility.* The facts show that investors, left to their own devices, will let their emotions make their decisions for them—and that these emotion-based decisions are often the primary cause of erratic returns. The ability to invest dispassionately by focusing on what is rational enables investors to avoid making mistakes that cost them dearly.

2. *Deliver great capabilities to all investment management decision making.* Good intentions—your own or those of any investment professionals you may work with—are not enough to maximize your chances of success. Indeed, most investors do not *intend* to follow advice that puts their portfolios in jeopardy. And yet this is exactly what many did by loading up on technology stocks during the late 1990s just before they came crashing down. Good intentions must be supplemented with the types of world-class capabilities and resources that are found only among the best investment institutions.

3. *Align your investment strategy with your long-term objectives and tolerance for risk.* Rational investors must accurately assess where they are today and where they want to go in order to determine the appropriate path they'll take toward achieving their goals. This requires identifying

crucial—but often overlooked—issues such as your objectives, the amount of financial resources you can commit, your time horizon, how much money you are comfortable losing without altering your investment plan, and an understanding of various types of investment risk. We'll explore how to align your strategy with your objectives and risk tolerance in Chapter 3. You'll also be introduced to the Investment Policy Statement, a written document based on your risk/return profile that provides a context for all future investment decisions. As you'll see, it is one of the most important tools an investor can have.

4. *Emphasize the importance of asset allocation.* The world's best institutional investors recognize a fact that may surprise you: The decision about which specific stocks, bonds, or other investments you select for your portfolio has little bearing on your returns. A much more important factor is how the dollars you invest are divided up among various types of broad asset categories—such as stocks, bonds, international investments, cash, and so on. Yet, despite its importance, few investors fully grasp the concept of asset allocation. Chapter 4 will shine a light on this often-misunderstood component of investing and show you how to implement a winning asset allocation strategy.

5. *Implement a plan using the appropriate investment vehicles.* Investors face a wide variety of choices when it comes to selecting the specific investment vehicles for their portfolios. However, we don't believe that building a portfolio of individual stocks on your own provides you with the great capabilities you need to succeed. Nor do we think that one type of investment is appropriate for all investors—a belief that flies in the face of many brokerage firms today that sell certain approaches, such as annuities or private money managers, to their clients regardless of their objectives or the amount of assets they can invest.

Instead, our process builds in the flexibility to ensure that you implement your unique plan using the investment vehicle that is most appropriate to your specific situation. The options we recommend in this book include a wide range of approaches used by clients of the top institutional investment firms: no-load mutual funds, variable annuities, exchange-traded funds, privately managed accounts, or a combination of these vehicles. You will learn how to decide which of these make the most sense for you, depending on the resources you have to commit.

6. *Monitor and adjust your portfolio on an ongoing basis.* Managing money intelligently requires you to take a dynamic approach to your portfolio. Unfortunately, investors often make the mistake of constructing their portfolios once but failing to revisit them regularly to make necessary adjustments.

   An institutional strategy, by contrast, places enormous importance on this crucial component of investing. Top institutional managers employ a comprehensive approach to monitoring and adjusting that delivers tremendous value and helps to ensure success. They systematically rebalance their exposure to asset classes such as stocks and bonds as market conditions change in order to maintain their desired balance between return potential and risk (a process called *strategic asset allocation*). Many also seek to enhance returns using *tactical asset allocation* strategies, in which managers opportunistically make subtle shifts to their portfolios when they identify areas of the market that their research indicates are over- or undervalued. These firms also regularly monitor investment managers in order to hold them accountable, asking such questions as: Is the manager with whom they invested assets still at the firm? Are the decision-making processes and capabilities still in place? And are they adding value by delivering competitive performance?

7. *Assess your progress regularly.* When your investment account statement arrives each month, do you read it? More important, do you understand what you read? We've learned from serving thousands of investors that a great number of you are frustrated because you don't know how to interpret these statements. As a result, many of you don't understand what investments you're holding, and even more of you don't know how to gauge your performance relative to an appropriate benchmark. Such confusion too often causes investors to make the wrong moves at the wrong times. Our process will reveal the techniques that top institutional investors use to

assess how they're progressing toward their goals and answer the question that's on every investor's mind: "How am I doing?"

We look forward to providing you with all that you need to achieve consistent investment success "on purpose." One important note: Throughout this book we cite several references to the historical performance of various indices, combinations of indices, and investment managers. These references are provided for illustrative purposes only. It is important to recognize that past performance is no guarantee of future results and that as an investor you cannot invest directly in an index.

Now let's get started!

NOTE

1. Represents a sample of institutional clients of our strategic alliance investment partners as of January 1, 2003. Inclusion on this list does not constitute an endorsement by any of these clients.

 **CHAPTER**

Investors Gone Bad: The Lessons of Behavioral Finance

*I*magine that you walked into your favorite department store or sporting goods shop to find it mobbed with shoppers desperately pulling items off the racks. As a harried clerk runs by, you flag him down. "Must be some sale you're running," you say.

The salesman looks at you incredulously. "Nope. We've actually marked up everything in the store by 50 percent. Better get in there with the rest of 'em before it's all gone."

Just as you're about to join the throngs of shoppers, you notice that the store across the street has signs in its window advertising 50 percent off all merchandise. But the store has no cars in the parking lot and no shoppers inside. "Gotta be something wrong with that place," you think as you begin indiscriminately grabbing whatever you can get your hands on.

Irrational? Ludicrous? You bet. In the real world, of course, we buy things when prices are low and watch for big sales so that we can stock up on our favorite items. No one in their right mind would do what the shoppers in the preceding example are doing— loading up on products when prices are sky high.

Well, almost no one. Time and time again, investors have shown a propensity to act like those crazed shoppers. We buy stocks, bonds, and other investments after their prices have soared because we want to get in on the action with other investors. Meanwhile, we systematically sell or ignore undervalued assets that are essentially "marked down," assuming that such low prices are a sign of shoddy merchandise.

In this chapter we'll take a closer look at the mistakes that investors make repeatedly and the damaging effects those mistakes have on the wealth-building process. We'll also explore the driving factors behind why investors make the decisions they do using Nobel Prize–winning research from the field of behavioral finance.

You'll find these insights to be of great value as you seek to make smarter decisions about your money. By understanding the mistakes that trip up investors and the psychology behind those mistakes, you'll be better able to stop making the types of poor investment decisions that threaten to derail your financial future. You'll also begin to understand the importance of adopting an institutional investment approach that removes emotions from the financial decision-making process so that you can design a successful investment plan and keep it on track.

THE CYCLE OF EMOTION

We like to think of ourselves as rational creatures in all that we do. When we make decisions, we evaluate the facts that are put in front of us in a thoughtful manner that allows us to make intelligent, informed choices. This capacity for critical thought is, after all, one of the biggest differences between human beings and less-evolved animals.

Unfortunately, our experience as investment advisors, as well as a growing body of academic research, tells us something very different. We have learned that investors, left to their own devices, systematically let their emotions override rational thought when it comes to deciding whether to buy or sell an investment. Instead of basing their decisions on empirical data such as a company's earnings growth rate and future prospects, the stock's valuation relative to the market or to comparable investments, their own tolerance for risk, and so on, investors get caught up in a wave of emotions that causes them to misinterpret the facts and make irrational investment decisions. The result: They make the wrong moves at the wrong times and risk failing to achieve their most important financial objectives.

Researchers have found that investors often go through a "cycle of emotion" that affects every aspect of an investment decision (see Exhibit 2-1).

EXHIBIT 2·1

The cycle of emotion. *(AssetMark Investment Services, Inc.)*

Using a hypothetical example of what happens to the typical investor who gets a hot stock tip, here's how this cycle of emotion causes us to make poor choices. Chances are you're a bit suspicious and don't race out right away and buy the stock—perhaps you've been burned in the past by a hot tip or maybe an extended market downturn has you doubting stocks in general. So you follow it occasionally. Sure enough, the stock price starts to move up, and doubt gives way to caution. You start tracking the stock's performance regularly and checking CNBC and financial magazines for mentions of the firm.

As the stock continues to rise, you become increasingly confident and enthusiastic that this could be the "big one"—the stock that makes you rich. Now the stock is getting more mentions in the media than ever. Meanwhile, analysts and market watchers aggressively promote this hot new story. The stock's trading volume soars, and its price-earnings (P/E) ratio hits uncharted territory. Suddenly you start to think that this winning stock just might make you so much money that you'll able to achieve your financial goals much faster than you anticipated.

At this point, enthusiasm turns to greed. Everyone is getting rich off the stock, and you can't bear the thought of being left out of the game. It no longer concerns you if the stock trades at 100 times projected earnings or that the company has yet to turn a profit: You want to be rich, and this is the stock that will get you there. To paraphrase Alan Greenspan, you have become "irrationally exuberant." That day, you buy the stock.

Anyone who's been in the markets during the past few years knows what happens next. The stock starts to fall shortly after your purchase. At first you're indifferent to the decline because you're probably still looking at a gain (on paper, anyway). As the stock continues to slide below your purchase price, you refuse to admit the possibility that the peak has been reached. You've got a loser on your hands but are emotionally unwilling to admit it. "It's a temporary setback, and I'm a long-term investor" is commonly heard at this point. "It'll bounce back in no time."

Instead, the stock price keeps sliding, and you start to feel concern and fear. It seems you've made a big mistake, and you promise yourself that if it just goes back to where you bought it, you'll never do it again. Making money is no longer the issue. You just want to break even so that you don't have to tell your spouse, friends, or accountant about your bad investment decision. Suddenly your fantasies of an early retirement or a second home seem like pipe dreams—in fact, this investment might just affect your entire financial well-being.

The selling pressure on the stock is now relentless. As the shares free fall and your financial picture looks grimmer, you lose the ability to assess the situation rationally. Wanting nothing more than relief from the stress of your present situation, you panic and sell—realizing a significant loss.

Then what happens? All too often new information comes out about the company, and the stock launches a big recovery. You bought at or near the top, only to hold on during the downturn just long enough to get scared and sell at the bottom.

Sound familiar? It will to many of you. Of course, we realize that some of you are right now protesting this entire idea of a cycle of emotion. "I'm smarter than that. I do my homework, pay attention to valuation, and invest for the long haul," you say. "I'm a rational investor."

If this is true, congratulations. But just to test your statement, ask yourself the following questions:

- *What did my portfolio look like in 1999 and 2000?* Did you load up on big-cap, household-name stocks? How much exposure did you have to the technology sector? And how did 3 consecutive years of heavy losses cause you to react—did you stay rational, or did panic take over?
- *What did my portfolio look like in 2002 and 2003?* Did you avoid or cash out of stocks despite the fact that equities were cheaper than they were 3 years earlier? Did the fixed-income market's hot performance prompt you to load up on bond funds, even though yields were anemic and the interest-rate risk in bonds was excessive?

The flow of new money into mutual fund categories during the past few years, shown in Exhibit 2-2, provides the answer. A great many of you were victims to the cycle of emotion, buying high because of greed and selling low because of fear. You piled into stocks at the wrong time, and then made the same mistake with bonds.

BEHAVIORAL FINANCE: WHY WE MAKE THE MISTAKES WE MAKE

We know that emotions too often drive the investment decision-making process for many investors. But why do we let our emotions replace rational investment processes in the first place? And just how devastating can these emotion-based decisions be to your financial picture?

A growing number of academics and other researchers have gone to great lengths to answer these very questions through a

EXHIBIT 2-2

Stock and bond fund flows.

Year	U.S. Stock Fund Net Inflows (billions)	Bond Fund Net Inflows (billions)
2002	−27.1	140.5
2001	31.9	87.7
2000	309.4	−49.8
1999	187.7	−4.1
1998	157.0	74.6

Source: Investment Company Institute, "Keep Your Eyes on the Road as You Look to Bond Funds," *Wall Street Journal,* February 3, 2003.

field of study called *behavioral finance,* which applies psychology to the investment process. These behaviorists reject the economic and financial theories that individuals act rationally by considering all available information when making decisions. Economic consultant Peter Bernstein sees "repeated patterns of irrationality, inconsistency, and incompetence in the ways human beings arrive at decisions and choices when faced with uncertainty."[1]

Behavioral finance seeks to explain the role of emotions in investors' actions. It's become an enormously useful and respected method to determine where we go wrong with our investment decisions. In fact, two early pioneers in the field, Princeton University's Daniel Kahneman and George Mason University's Vernon Smith, received the 2002 Nobel Prize in economics for their behavioral finance research.

The overall theme found in behavioral finance is that the circuitry in our brains is "wired" in such a way as to cause us to make costly investment mistakes. In other words, it's normal for us to get caught up in emotions, second guess our allocation to various asset classes, and make inappropriate changes to our portfolios that boost risk and reduce returns. "We're only human," say behaviorists. "We're bound to make mistakes."

RULES OF THUMB LEAD TO BAD DECISIONS

Behaviorists have learned that one main reason we fail as investors is that we rely on faulty "rules of thumb" to guide our decisions. This tendency is, unfortunately, a part of who we are as human beings. Our brains naturally want to forecast the future based on past experiences. Take an example such as gambling in a casino. A roll of the dice or a spin of the roulette wheel is a random act—yet we're positive we can discern patterns that tell us that the next roll will be a seven or that red is due to come up.

Perhaps the most pervasive and harmful rule of thumb that works its way into investors' minds (despite what is written on every prospectus) is the following: *Past performance is the best predictor of future returns.* Our brains are constantly on the lookout for patterns, and it thinks it identifies them quite quickly. Research by Duke University neuroscientist Scott Huettel reveals that it takes only two similar events for the brain to expect that event to occur again.[2] Based on this evidence, it would take only 2 years of strong performance from a mutual fund for a typical investor to assume that the fund's hot streak will continue.

This natural tendency of our brains explains why study after study shows that investors choose their mutual funds based on performance. Investors constantly chase hot funds, believing that great returns over a 6-month or 1-year period is a clear sign that the manager is skilled (not lucky, as so many turn out to be). And of course, mutual fund managers are often rewarded for posting the best short-term results and fired if they don't—so it clearly pays for them to promote this short-term performance game.

In fact, fund companies often go as far as setting up incubator funds to "juice" their overall performance records. These funds are run by the company but are not available to the public unless they deliver strong returns over a period of a few years—at which point the fund company opens the funds to retail investors and advertises their stellar performance. The sole purpose of these funds is to have at least one offering with terrific numbers that the company can market aggressively to investors hungry for the next hot ticket.

This assumption that any investment manager's performance over a limited time period indicates its likely performance going forward has been proven repeatedly to be absolutely false. Some of the most compelling evidence we've seen comes from one of our strategic institutional investment partners, investment consulting firm Wilshire Associates. By examining a large "universe" of managers that run both mutual funds and institutional accounts, they identified the small-cap value managers that performed in the top quartile (top 25 percent) of their category during the 5 years ending 1997 and tracked their performances for the following 5 years.

Wilshire's findings show that past performance is, in fact, an extremely poor predictor of future results. Of the managers that delivered top-quartile returns during the first 5-year period, just 21 percent managed to do the same during the second 5-year period. Amazingly, a full 50 percent of these managers posted bottom-quartile (i.e., the worst possible) returns (see Exhibit 2-3).

Brandes Investment Partners, an institutional investment firm that we have worked with for many years, found a similar dynamic among stocks whose prices had fallen by 60 percent or more during a period of 1 year or less. These so-called falling-knife stocks are steadfastly avoided by most investors, who assume that the firms will soon go bankrupt or be delisted. Money managers are especially unwilling to buy these stocks, fearing that their bosses

EXHIBIT 2-3

The problem with chasing performance. *(Wilshire Associates.)*

Wilshire Small-Cap Value Universe Performance

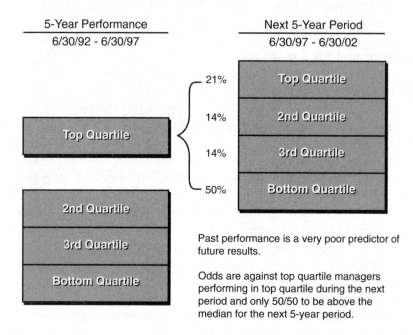

5-Year Performance
6/30/92 - 6/30/97

Next 5-Year Period
6/30/97 - 6/30/02

Past performance is a very poor predictor of future results.

Odds are against top quartile managers performing in top quartile during the next period and only 50/50 to be above the median for the next 5-year period.

will fire them for holding such clear losers. The conventional wisdom on Wall Street says to "Never catch a falling knife."

However, Brandes discovered that these stocks present opportunities for investors who think rationally. Falling knives, on average, outperformed the Standard & Poor's (S&P) 500 by 10.9 percentage points in the year following their declines, 13.6 percentage points annually in the following 2 years, and 8.6 percentage points annually during the 3 years after their fall (see Exhibit 2-4). Once again, it is clear that recent past performance is a thoroughly unreliable signpost for the road ahead.

MORE BAD BEHAVIOR

The evidence reveals that following faulty rules of thumb enough times can devastate your chances of achieving the financial success and freedom you desire. In a landmark study entitled, "Investors

EXHIBIT 2·4

Average annualized outperformance of falling knives (based on returns from 1091 falling knives in the United States between 1986 and 2003). *(Brandes Institute, a division of Brandes Investment Partners.)*

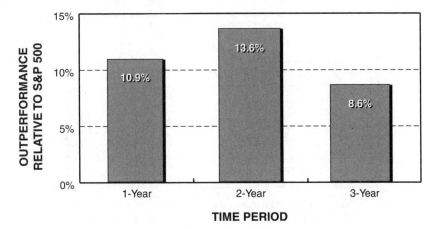

TIME PERIOD

Behaving Badly," Financial Research Corporation found that mutual fund investors consistently underperform the very funds in which they invest by an average of 2.2 percentage points annually (see Exhibit 2-5). Think about this the next time you read about a fund's stellar returns in a financial publication.

The damage of missing a mere 2.2 percentage points of performance can be substantial, perhaps even enough to affect your lifestyle. A $100,000 investment in a fund earning 10.9 percent annually would grow to roughly $791,828 in 20 years (not accounting for taxes). By contrast, an investor who earned an 8.7 percent return annually during that time would end up with $530,385—a difference of $261,443.

So why do investors underperform so significantly? Essentially it's because they allow their emotions to dictate their decisions and abandon their investment strategies. They do this by trading too frequently and by chasing after those investments and asset classes that have delivered strong recent performance.

These tendencies can be seen in the research. Investors are jumping in and out of funds far more frequently than they realize or care to admit—and harming their chances of financial success in the process. Financial Research Corporation concluded that fund investors' holding period—the amount of time they own shares in

EXHIBIT 2-5

Investors underperform their own funds (represents average annual mutual fund returns versus dollar-weighted mutual fund investor returns for the time period January 1990 to December 2000). *(Financial Research Corporation.)*

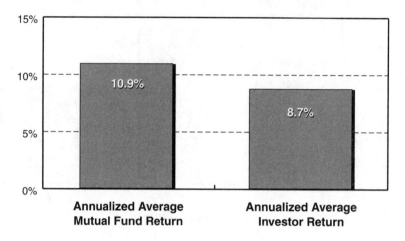

Annualized Average Mutual Fund Return   **Annualized Average Investor Return**

a fund—would have to be 10 years in order for the investors to accurately be described as long term. However, they discovered that the average holding period for mutual funds is a mere 2.9 years (see Exhibit 2-6).

Translation: Average investors hold onto their funds for *less than* 3 years. In no way can such short holding periods be deemed long-term investing.

Of course, excessive turnover may add value if investors consistently were able to shift money out of investments that were overpriced and due for a fall and into undervalued assets with significant upside potential. Unfortunately, most investors do the exact opposite: Their emotional responses to market movements, as well as their "prewired" tendencies to find meaningful patterns in random short-term events, cause them to invest heavily in assets that have delivered exceptionally strong recent performance and are set to deliver lower returns going forward. Likewise, they avoid or sell those investments which have underperformed in the short term but are on track to produce increasingly greater future returns. Just like our hypothetical shoppers, investors buy high and sell low.

For proof, look at the year 2000. Investors poured $4.1 billion into technology funds during the 6 months following the Nasdaq's

EXHIBIT 2-6

Why investors underperform—turnover temptation.

Year	Implied Holding Period (years)
1996	5.5
1997	5.0
1998	4.8
1999	3.6
2000	2.9

Source: Financial Research Corporation for the 5 years ending December 31, 2000.

peak.[3] And as Exhibit 2-2 showed, investors withdrew nearly $50 billion from bond funds that same year, just as bonds were beginning an extended period of outperformance.

"Investors Behaving Badly" reveals just how badly investors who chase performance suffer. The average return of 48 Morningstar fund categories (unweighted returns) was almost always higher than the returns achieved by investors in those categories during 1-, 2-, and 3-year periods from January 1990 through March 2000 (see Exhibit 2-7). In fact, investors underperformed the very funds in which they invested in approximately 80 to 90 percent of the Morningstar categories.

We are especially amazed by how *consistently* investors buy the wrong things at the wrong times. Financial Research Corporation examined the flow of new money into various fund categories following their best and worst periods of performance (summarized in Exhibit 2-8). Across all Morningstar categories, the average quarterly return in the best four quarters was 14 percent, as opposed to –9 percent in the worst four quarters. Following the best quarters—that is, after the funds had already posted huge gains—mutual fund inflows were $91 billion. After the worst quarters—when the funds had fallen and offered better value— fund inflows were a mere $6.5 billion.

A closer look reveals some startling disparities. For example, inflows into large-cap growth funds following that category's best four quarters were $20.6 billion. After the category's worst four quarters, however, inflows dropped to $5.1 billion—a difference of $15.5 billion. Who says investors' emotions don't cause them to chase performance?

EXHIBIT 2-7

Buying high, selling low.

	1-Year	2-Year	3-Year
Number of investment categories in which category returns surpassed investors' actual returns (of 48 categories)	37	42	37
Percentage of investment categories in which category returns surpassed investors' actual returns	77%	88%	77%

Source: Financial Research Corporation.

EXHIBIT 2-8

Mutual fund inflows following best and worst quarters.

Category	Best Four Quarters' Returns	Next Quarter's Net Sales (millions)	Worst Four Quarters' Returns	Next Quarter's Net Sales (millions)
Large blend	16.30%	13,158	−8.57%	7148
Large growth	22.16%	20,556	−8.67%	5070
Large value	13.79%	4283	−9.70%	2943
Midcap blend	17.53%	−39	−10.93%	−112
Midcap growth	27.09%	7944	−13.86%	−108
Midcap value	13.68%	−1662	−10.91%	−2687
Small blend	18.00%	411	−13.89%	84
Small growth	27.37%	3113	−15.76%	827
Small blend	17.29%	1630	−14.05%	−874

Source: Financial Research Corporation.

FORM OVER SUBSTANCE: THE EFFECTS OF FRAMING

Behavioral finance also tells us that investors are highly influenced by how a problem (such as an investment or an outcome of investing) is presented—or *framed*—versus what the problem truly is. In other words, the way an investment is presented to you (the form) can play a bigger role in your decision about that investment than its true nature (the substance). If you've ever bought a stock because it had a great story, you'll understand the concept of framing. It's yet another way in which investors systematically ignore objective factors, such as the risk and return tradeoff between investments, when making their decisions.

Research into framing by Daniel Kahneman and Amos Tversky tells us that investors place different weights on gains and losses, as well as on different ranges of probability. As investors, we are more distressed by the potential for losses than we are happy about the potential for equivalent gains. Some economists believe that investors think losing one dollar is twice as painful as the pleasure they receive from gaining one dollar. Does this accurately describe your feelings toward gains and losses?

As a result of this psychological factor, investors will react differently to equivalent situations depending on whether those situations are framed with a focus on losses or a focus on gains. Specifically, you are more likely to take risks to avoid losses than to achieve gains. As Exhibit 2-9 shows, we become risk takers when faced with sure loss. But when given the opportunity for sure gain, we try to avoid risk.

Framing, therefore, can cause you to react in exactly the wrong way when, say, rebalancing your investment portfolio. Instead of cutting back on your best-performing and potentially overvalued investments and increasing your exposure to those holdings which have underperformed recently and offer value, you'll be tempted to do the opposite: Let your winners ride and cut your losses.

If we feel worse about prospective losses than happy about equivalent gains, we are also more likely to hold losing investments

---

EXHIBIT 2-9

Framing leads to substantially different outcomes.

Groups of subjects were presented with a number of problems.

One group was presented with this problem:
In addition to whatever you own, you have been given $1000. You are now asked to choose between
a. A sure gain of $500.
b. A 50 percent chance to gain $1000 and a 50 percent chance to gain nothing.

The other group was given this problem:

In addition to whatever you own, you have been given $2000. You are now asked to choose between
a. A sure loss of $500.
b. A 50 percent chance to lose $1000 and a 50 percent chance to lose nothing.

In the first group, 84 percent chose a. In the second group, 68 percent chose b. The two problems are identical in terms of net cash to the subject, but the phrasing of the questions causes the problems to be interpreted differently.

Source: Daniel Kahneman and Amos Tversky, "Prospect Theory: An Analysis of Decision Making Under Risk," *Econometrica*, 47 (1979): 263-291

too long and sell winning investments too soon—a behavioral finance concept known as the *disposition effect.*

University of California–Davis Finance Professor Brad Barber found that between February 1991 and January 1997, the disposition effect resulted in investors earning returns that were 3.58 percentage points lower than the return of the S&P 500. In the Silicon Valley, near where our corporate headquarters are located, we've seen this disposition effect in action for several years among thousands of technology executives who held onto their tech stocks as they continued to plummet. We have yet to find the investor who didn't fall victim to this type of behavior when it came to technology stocks.

Behaviorists tell us that one reason we're so reluctant to sell our poorest performing investments is because we seek to avoid feeling regret. For example, when you decide whether or not to sell a stock, you're typically emotionally affected by whether you bought it for more or less than the current price. By selling stocks that have fallen below the purchase price, you have to face up to the pain that comes with admitting that you made an error in judgment. You've locked in a loss that came about from your own poor choices.

These and other behavioral finance concepts are being studied and used by an increasing number of leading members of the investment community. Many investors now believe that the errors investors make due to their emotions and "prewired" psychologies actually can cause mispricing in the financial markets. In contrast to the belief that markets are efficient, these investors look for ways in which investors' mistakes lead to inefficiencies in the markets that can be exploited for profit. In fact, several world-class investment strategists with whom we work—including Litman/Gregory Asset Management and PanAgora Asset Management—have achieved significant success by incorporating the lessons of behavioral finance into their investment management strategies.

BREAKING THE CYCLE

As we've seen, the emotions and behavioral factors that affect the very workings of our brains—such as faulty rules of thumb and framing—cause investors to make poor and extremely costly investment decisions over and over again:

- Although we say that we are long-term investors (and even if we truly believe it), we will react to short-term influences.

- We want to invest in asset classes that currently are performing well.
- We want to avoid or sell asset classes that currently are not performing well.

One way to become a more successful investor, therefore, is to avoid making these types of mistakes. This may sound like a tall order given all the empirical evidence we've seen showing that investors are predisposed to errors in judgment when it comes to their finances. The truth is that it is difficult to overcome our emotions and innate reactions—especially when they concern our own hard-earned money.

The good news is that you can break the cycle of emotion-based investing and the resulting negative impacts on your portfolio. The key is to adopt a disciplined investment approach that replaces emotion with a proven, rational process, as well as the capabilities that will enable you to stick with that approach despite the market's behavior in the short run. As you read the next six chapters, you'll learn all that we know about the type of institutional process that will enable you to enjoy a lifetime of investment success.

NOTES

1. Bernstein, Peter, *Against the Gods: The Remarkable Story of Risk (New York*: Wiley, 1998).
2. Huettel, Scott, Peter Mack, and Gregory McCarthy, "Perceiving Patterns in Random Series: Dynamic Processing of Sequence in Prefrontal Cortex." Manuscript, Duke University, Durham, NC, April 2002.
3. "Mutual Funds Change Monikers, But Not Holdings, to Woo Money," *Wall Street Journal*, March 14, 2003.

Financial Analysis: Your First Step to Investment Success

*I*nvestors often want to dive headfirst into the investment process by deciding which stocks or funds to buy for their portfolios. This is understandable. Such decisions are what make investing exciting for many investors. Before you can get to those steps, however, it is necessary to undergo a process of financial analysis that will shape all your investment decisions to come.

We believe that the path to investment success always begins with an honest assessment of three crucial financial issues that affect all investors:

- Where are you today?
- Where do you want to be in the future?
- How will you get there?

These questions suggest an important fact about successful investing that investors sometimes forget. You don't start by looking outward to specific investments or managers. Instead, you begin by being introspective about your own goals, resources, and needs so that you can build a plan for being successful "on purpose." The world's biggest pension plans, endowments, and other large investors always begin by assessing these issues—in fact, many of them hire consulting firms to guide them through this very process because they believe it is so important.

Your job as an investor looking to make the smartest possible decisions about your money is to incorporate the proven approaches used by these large investors. This means that your first step is to draw up a financial roadmap that takes into account your goals, your current financial picture, and the appropriate path to take toward achieving all that is important to you. The importance of such a roadmap can't be overstated. The investment decisions you make ultimately will affect your quality of life—as well as the quality of life enjoyed by your family and heirs—over the coming decades. You owe it to yourself and to them to make wise decisions at every step.

In this chapter we'll show you how to start out on the right foot by building an overall structure for your investing that will allow you to maximize your probability of achieving your goals.

THE INVESTMENT POLICY STATEMENT: THE CENTER OF YOUR INVESTMENT PLAN

As with any investment in life, you significantly boost your chances of achieving the best results if you carefully construct a plan that helps you to make smart decisions and stick to them over time. When it comes to investing your financial assets, one of the most powerful tools to boost your probability of success is a written investment plan. Large pension plans have used these plans, known as *Investment Policy Statements,* for decades to successfully guide their strategies. Until recently, however, most individual investors—even those working with professional financial advisors—have not taken advantage of this tool. Because we believe that your key to success is to incorporate the best practices of world-class investors, we strongly encourage you to build your own comprehensive Investment Policy Statement. In fact, the advisors we work with prepare this document for every one of their clients.

A written investment plan is the end result of performing a financial self-assessment to determine where you are, where you want to be, and the best path to get there. It addresses such factors as your goals and specific circumstances, your time horizon, your comfort with investment risk, and the investment strategies that you will follow.

By putting all this information in writing, you'll be perfectly clear on the long-term goals you hope to achieve by investing. As a result, you'll be better able to maintain your plan both in good markets (when greed may tempt you to load up on hot market sectors) and bad (when short-term declines may cause you to doubt your approach). As we learned in Chapter 2, investors easily get caught up in the emotions of the marketplace. An Investment Policy Statement that outlines how your portfolio will be managed not only will put your smart decisions on paper—it also will serve as a reminder of your carefully crafted strategy during volatile markets so that you don't make emotional mistakes.

Every Investment Policy Statement should include the following six topics. We'll detail some of these topics now and focus on others—such as asset allocation and portfolio rebalancing—in later chapters. By the end of this book, you'll know how to incorporate all the crucial elements of a financial plan into your Investment Policy Statement.

1. Set your long-term needs, objectives, and values.
2. Establish your time horizon.
3. Determine your rate-of-return objective and select the asset classes.
4. Define the level of risk you can accept.
5. Document the investment methodology.
6. Establish a strategic implementation plan.

CLARIFYING YOUR VALUES AND GOALS

Long-term investment success means different things to different people. Some of us need to fund college educations for our children, whereas others are concerned primarily with having enough money to live comfortably in retirement or donate to our favorite charities. Therefore, the best investment plan for you depends on your unique values and objectives. The first task in financial analysis is to uncover those values and objectives so that you're clear about what you're trying to accomplish. Ask yourself such questions as

- What would I like my top accomplishments to be?
- What are my personal and professional goals?
- What family member relationships are most important to me?
- What do I want for my children? My parents? Other family members?
- Ideally, where would I like to be when I am 45? 55? 65? 75?
- How much money do I need or want (in dollar terms)?

- What would I like my investments to achieve?
- When I think about my money, what concerns, needs, or feelings come to mind?

You may find it difficult to set goals that you are willing to work toward consistently, but it's important that you take this step. Without an "end game" in mind, you can be distracted easily from saving and investing for your own future and make poor financial decisions that end up affecting your quality of life down the road. The key is to set goals that are extremely meaningful to you so that you're motivated to focus on them even if they're years or decades away. Meaningful goals will always reflect your own set of core values—those elements of your life which are most important to you.

DETERMINING YOUR TIME HORIZON

Once you define your goals, you must determine how long your money must work for you in order to achieve those goals. If you're like most investors, you'll need your assets to grow for many decades. Certainly, young investors just starting to save for retirement and other goals require very long time horizons. However, so will recently retired workers, who must ensure that their money sustains them throughout a retirement that may last 20 years or longer.

Ideally, your long-term time horizon should be as far into the future as possible in order to take full advantage of the effects of compound growth on your investments. Compound growth essentially means that you earn money not just on the capital you invest but also on your investment returns. The positive effects of this process on your wealth increase the longer you allow it to work for you.

In fact, the amount of time you let your money grow will have a bigger effect on your wealth than the amount of money you invest. Consider Investor A, 20 years old, who invests $5000 a year for 10 years in a portfolio that earns 8 percent annually. At age 30, this investor stops investing new money. Assuming that the portfolio continues to earn 8 percent per year on average, Investor A will end up with $1,156,619 at age 65. By contrast, Investor B begins investing $5000 a year starting at age 40 and continues to invest for 25 years, until age 65. Despite having invested 2.5 times the amount of money as Investor A, Investor B winds up with just $394,772 at retirement—a difference of more than $760,000.

A longer time horizon also helps to reduce investment risk. Exhibit 3-1 shows the returns over time of the Standard & Poor's

(S&P) 500, an index of 500 large U.S. stocks. Note how returns can swing wildly over short periods such as 1 year but tend to become much more predictable over the long term. Over long periods, the ups and downs of the market largely cancel each other out, making for a smoother ride. In fact, no investor who has held stocks during any 20-year period since 1926 has lost money in the S&P 500.

WHERE YOU STAND NOW

A second component of building your comprehensive financial plan is to determine where you currently stand financially in relation to your values-based goals. This essentially tells you your starting point and how many miles you'll need to travel on your journey to financial success.

At this stage you'll conduct a self-assessment of your net worth, the amount of investable assets available to fund your goals, the percentage of your income that you can earmark to those goals going forward, and your liquidity needs. Answering the following questions will give you a good idea of your current financial scenario:

- What is my source of income (business, employer, profession, and so on)?
- How do I make money today (including bonuses, commissions, dividends, interest, rental income, and so on)? How will this likely change in the next 3 years?
- What percentage of my income do I set aside to invest? How is this likely to change in the next 3 years?
- What benefits do I receive from my workplace?
- What are my investment holdings (including retirement plans, savings, stocks, bonds, mutual funds, investment real estate, and so on)? How are they currently structured?

EXHIBIT 3-1

S&P 500 Index overlapping returns, 1926–2002 (annualized).

	1 Year	5 Years	10 Years	20 Years
Highest return	54.0%	28.6%	20.1%	17.9%
Annualized return	10.2%	10.6%	11.1%	11.3%
Lowest return	−43.3%	−12.5%	−0.9%	3.1%

Source: Ibbotson Associates.

- What are my current liabilities (mortgage, credit cards, auto loans, and so on)?
- What new assets, if any, do I expect to receive (from stock options, inheritance, and so on)?
- How much money do I have in liquid reserves for emergencies? Three to six months' worth of living expenses should be sufficient for most people.
- My tax situation: Am I in a high-income tax bracket? Do I currently hold a portfolio of highly appreciated securities that stands to get hit with a heavy tax bill if I sell?

CLOSING THE GAP

The gap between where you are now and where you want to be down the road will be coming into focus at this point. Investors typically find a fairly wide chasm between the two points. Because our goals and aspirations tend to rise along with our wealth, even investors with millions of dollars can find themselves relatively far away from where they seek to be. To close the gap, you'll need to know how hard your money must work for you over your expected time horizon, as well as the risks that you'll face in the process.

Estimating Your Rate of Return

To reach your goals, your portfolio needs to achieve a high enough rate of return over time to satisfy your objectives. Numerous software tools now allow you to calculate rate-of-return objectives. The most basic include any number of financial calculators available on the Internet (see the box below for a list of some of the best). Although these Web-based calculators may not be as advanced as those used by professional investors, they provide do-it-yourselfers with reasonable estimates to use in an investment plan.

More advanced software that offers Monte Carlo simulation, which is being used increasingly by financial advisors, can provide a deeper level of analysis about your portfolio's expected return. Monte Carlo simulation calculates not just the necessary rate of return but also the probability that you'll actually achieve that rate of return. The software relies on advanced computer modeling technology that factors in thousands of different possible year-by-year returns, including long stretches in which the markets post returns well below their historical averages.

The rate of return you actually achieve will be determined largely by the types of assets you include in your portfolio and the manner in which you combine them. We'll explore these issues in Chapter 4. Generally speaking, however, the higher your required rate of return, the more money you'll need to allocate to stocks (which historically have delivered the strongest returns over time). (See Exhibit 3-2.)

Your analysis may suggest that you require a return that is essentially unattainable based on the long-term returns of various asset classes. If you have a very large financial goal but only a small sum to invest toward it, for example, you may find that you need a rate of return in excess of 20 percent per year. In this case you must reassess your financial scenario and ask yourself

- *Can I invest more money toward my goals?* Boosting your savings rate and contributing more money to your investment plan can help you to close the gap significantly. Consider that an extra $1000 invested monthly would grow to nearly $600,000 after 20 years, assuming an 8 percent annualized return.
- *Can I push back my goals for a few years?* As we've seen above, the benefits of compounding increase dramatically the longer you allow your investments to work for you.

EXHIBIT 3-2

Rates of return for asset classes (1926–2002).

Asset Class	Annualized Long-Term Return
Small-cap stocks	12.2%
Large-cap stocks	10.2%
Long-term government bonds	5.5%
Treasury bills	3.8%

Source: Ibbotson Associates.

- *Do I need to rethink my goals?* You may find that you need to adjust your goals downward—a less expensive college for your children, a smaller home, or a more modest retirement income, for example.

Understanding Risk

An investment plan is incomplete without an understanding and assessment of risk. If you don't recognize the types of risk you face as an investor—as well as the amount of risk you're comfortable with—short-term market events probably will cause you to over-react and make emotional decisions that can wreak havoc on your financial future.

There are four major types of investment risk that affect all investors:

- *Market risk.* This is the risk associated with being an investor in a particular market, such as the stock market or bond market. If you invest in stocks, for example, you must accept the fact that their prices will fall temporarily from time to time. In fact, stock price fluctuations over short periods can be especially severe: As we saw in Exhibit 3-1, an investor holding stocks for just 1 year could have had returns as high as 54 percent and as low as –43 percent. In Chapter 4 you'll see how diversifying across different asset classes that don't move in lockstep with each other is the most effective way to reduce the impact of market risk on your wealth.
- *Financial risk.* Also called *company-specific risk,* this is the risk you take by owning a particular stock or other security. Individual stocks often fall due to company-specific factors

even as the market as a whole rises. Investors in Boston Market learned this lesson painfully. Exhibit 3-3 shows that shares of the restaurant chain went into free fall during the late 1990s as the S&P 500 soared. You can best mitigate financial risk by diversifying among at least 30 different stocks. In this way your fortunes aren't tied to the fate of a single firm.

- *Inflation risk.* This occurs when you invest in assets with rates of return that are too low to counter the effects of rising prices on the value of your money. Many investors are tempted to hold only "safe" assets, such as short-term bonds or cash, that don't fluctuate in value as much as stocks. The trouble is that a portfolio consisting of bonds and cash is at the mercy of inflation because these types of assets historically have had a hard time keeping pace with rising prices.

  Inflation's effect on your savings can be even worse than a market meltdown. The value of $1 million today will fall to around $440,000 in 20 years, assuming a modest 4 percent inflation rate. The upshot: To earn positive returns after inflation, you must include equities in your portfolio.

- *Goals-oriented risk.* We believe that the biggest risk you face is the risk of not having sufficient investment capital to meet your long-term goals. Think about never accumulating enough money to retire and being forced to work your entire life to get by. This risk is considerably more dangerous than the risk of your portfolio temporarily declining in value for a period of a few months or years. It's also what drives smart investors to build plans that are focused squarely on achieving specific, well-defined goals. To combat this risk, you'll need to include stocks in your portfolio in order to both stay ahead of inflation and provide the growth you need to reach your objectives.

Assessing Your Risk Tolerance

Investors can do much to minimize the preceding risks, but they cannot eliminate them completely. You must face the fact that over the course of your investment life, your portfolio's value will rise and fall.

EXHIBIT 3-3

Financial risk—Boston Market versus S&P 500. (*BigCharts.*)

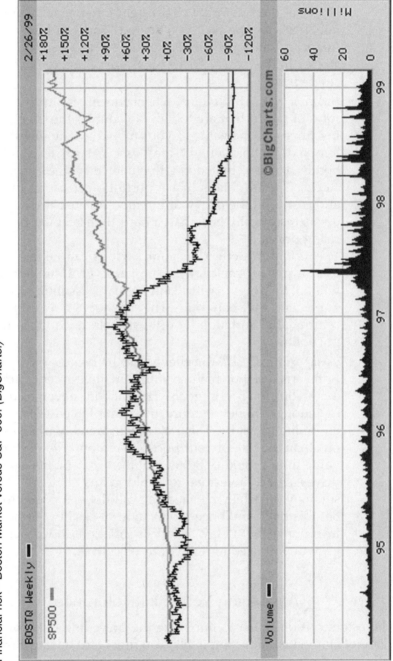

It's imperative, therefore, to determine your own risk tolerance—the amount of risk that you're comfortable taking in your plan. If you align your plan with your risk tolerance, you'll be able to maintain your strategy in both strong and weak markets. If you don't, periods of extreme losses will tempt you to ditch your plan at exactly the wrong moments.

Your risk tolerance is determined by your level of comfort during those periods when your portfolio's value declines. It's done by assessing the amount of short-term losses you're willing to accept in pursuit of long-term objectives without terminating your plan. Our approach to determining risk tolerance is to ask clients quantitative-based questions to uncover their appetite for short-term dips in the value of their accounts.

In particular, ask yourself, "What's the worst 1-year return I could stand without abandoning my strategy?" To help answer this question and determine your own risk tolerance, consider Exhibit 3-4. It shows six risk/return profiles, each representing a portfolio with a different degree of exposure to equities. Although it lists the average return and best return during 1-year rolling periods, pay close attention to the worst 1-year returns. These figures

EXHIBIT 3-4

Six risk/return profiles.

Risk/Return Profile	Percent in Stocks	Average Annual Return	Best 1-Year Return	Worst 1-Year Return
Capital preservation	20%	9.81%	33.39%	−13.35%
Balanced income	40%	10.59%	40.23%	−20.51%
Balanced	60%	11.25%	43.95%	−27.22%
Balanced growth	75%	11.80%	47.62%	−32.11%
Growth	90%	12.35%	52.44%	−36.74%
Aggressive growth	98%	12.57%	59.52%	−38.80%

Note: This information has been compiled by AssetMark Investment Services, Inc., to reflect the historical returns from January 1, 1973 to December 31, 2002, of the following combinations of indices used to construct the multi-asset class benchmarks for risk/return profiles from capital preservation to aggressive growth. Capital preservation: 20 percent Wilshire 5000, 78 percent Lehman Brothers Intermediate Aggregate Bond, 2 percent cash; balanced income: 30 percent Wilshire 5000, 10 percent MSCI EAFE, 58 percent, Lehman Brothers Aggregate Bond, 2 percent cash; balanced: 40 percent Wilshire 5000, 20 percent MSCI EAFE, 38 percent, Lehman Brothers Aggregate Bond, 2 percent cash; balanced growth: 50 percent Wilshire 5000, 25 percent MSCI EAFE, 23 percent Lehman Brothers Aggregate Bond, 2 percent cash; growth: 60 percent Wilshire 5000, 30 percent MSCI EAFE, 8 percent Lehman Brothers Aggregate Bond, 2 percent cash; aggressive growth: 59 percent Wilshire 5000, 39 percent MSCI EAFE, 2 percent cash. Performance is based on rolling periods. Returns in excess of 1 year are annualized. Where the time period analyzed precedes the inception of a benchmark, the "best fit" index was used. There is no guarantee that the objective return of any profile will be achieved. Past performance is no guarantee of future results. Investors cannot invest directly in an index.

Source: AssetMark Investment Services, December 2002.

are often quite sobering for investors. You may define yourself as an aggressive investor who doesn't mind volatility—but what if your portfolio lost nearly 40 percent in just 12 months? Could you stomach such a dramatic decline?

Before you answer, consider the question from another angle. If you had a portfolio worth $1 million and its value fell to $612,000 in the course of 1 year, would you be able to stick with your portfolio—or even invest more money in it? If not, you need to move down the risk/reward spectrum to a portfolio that offers potentially less volatility.

DETERMINING YOUR INVOLVEMENT

A final consideration when building your investment plan has to do with your attitudes toward investing and whether you need or desire assistance. Ask yourself these two questions:

- How involved do I want to be in the investing process?
- Who else do I want involved in my financial planning (e.g., a spouse, child, or advisor)?

Clearly, a big part of your financial success will be your ability to stay focused on your goals, return objectives, and risk tolerance. Some investors find that they have the time, training, and temperament to handle these matters themselves or in combination with trusted family members. Other investors find that they lack the skills needed to implement and maintain a successful investment plan. Some simply don't care to be involved intimately in their financial decision making. And there are those of you who have a lot more money than time. These investors often prefer to delegate the responsibility of consultative financial planning to an advisor.

For those of you who are considering working with an advisor, it is important to find one who has adopted the type of disciplined processes described in this book (see Chapter 15 for advice on how to size up advisors).

At this point you're ready to move to the next step: Dividing your investment capital among major asset categories such as stocks, bonds, and cash. Asset allocation is one of the most important decisions you'll make as an investor—and in Chapter 4 we'll show you how the best investors in the world do it.

Asset Allocation: Getting the Right Mix

The concept of asset allocation has existed for several decades, and its basic message has become well established in the investment community. By building diversified portfolios consisting of multiple asset classes (such as U.S. and international stocks, bonds, and cash), investors stand the best chance of achieving their financial goals without exposing themselves to undue risk.

Yet, despite the attention that's been given to asset allocation over the years, it remains one of the most misunderstood and underused components of investing. If every investor truly understood and practiced sound asset allocation strategies, no one would invest the bulk of their retirement savings in their employer's stock, as so many workers do through their 401(k) plans. And certainly no one would make the mistake of buying a dozen different technology stocks and calling themselves well-diversified investors—a common practice during the late 1990s that caused a staggering amount of wealth to be lost in the ensuing years.

Your duty as an investor looking to make the smartest possible decisions is to understand the vital role that asset allocation plays in your future investment success and to incorporate the most advanced asset allocation techniques that can maximize your chances of achieving your goals. We believe that the decision about how to build a diversified portfolio using carefully selected asset classes is one of the most important choices you'll ever make during your lifetime as an investor. Our goal is to show you how it's done by the best investment minds in the world.

THE IMPORTANCE OF ASSET ALLOCATION

The first questions many investors ask when they start building or revamping their investment portfolios are "What stocks should I buy?" and "Which mutual funds should I pick?" Their focus is entirely on selecting the securities that will go into their portfolios. Given the thousands of stocks and funds in existence, investors can—and regularly do—spend extraordinary amounts of time trying to answer these questions.

Trouble is, these aren't the most important questions to ask. The first question always must be "How will I allocate my assets among the major asset classes?" The reason for this is quite simple: The asset classes you choose and the percentage of your portfolio that you earmark to each one likely will have a greater impact on your portfolio's future returns than any other decision.

The importance of asset allocation to investors' returns has been well documented in a landmark study conducted by some of the world's most revered investment experts. These experts studied the returns of 91 large pension funds from 1974 through 1983 to measure scientifically which factors were most important in determining investment performance.

The results of their research fundamentally reshaped how investors manage money. On average, a full 91 percent of the variations in returns of the portfolios studied could be explained by asset allocation—how the assets were divided among different types of asset classes. By contrast, the traditional area where investors focus their time and attention—selecting individual securities—explained surprisingly little of the return variations (see Exhibit 4-1).

To illustrate just how powerful a force asset allocation is in explaining the variability of portfolio performance, consider a hypothetical investor who bought a portfolio of a dozen large-cap technology stocks in 1997. That investor would have realized enormous gains during the next 3 years—not because the investor was a world-class stock picker but because the overwhelming majority of big-cap tech shares were on a tear. Likewise, that same portfolio would have come crashing down during the following 3 years, resulting in a very unpleasant roller coaster ride for the investor. However, this volatile ride had little to do with the individual stocks the investor held. Instead, the investors' asset allocation—the decision to invest entirely in one asset class—was responsible for the variability of the performance.

EXHIBIT 4-1

Asset allocation's importance. *(Financial Analyst Journal, May–June 1991.)*

For investors looking to maximize the probability of achieving their goals, the lesson of the study is clear: Once you've determined your risk tolerance, time horizon, and long-term objectives, most of the time you spend on your investments should be devoted to making smart asset allocation decisions. Your goal should be to use advanced asset allocation strategies—the kind used by the investment community's top minds—when designing and maintaining your own investment portfolio.

ADVANCED ASSET ALLOCATION: A NOBEL PRIZE–WINNING APPROACH

While most discussions of asset allocation are summed up using the often-cited cliché of "Don't put all your eggs in one basket," advanced asset allocation provides you with a more sophisticated approach. It uses proven mathematical formulas to determine which asset classes are most appropriate for you to own, as well as the optimal way to combine those asset classes to give you the maximum diversification benefits. Essentially, advanced asset allocation answers two crucial questions that every investor should ask: Which asset classes should I choose and how much of each asset class should I hold?

Advanced asset allocation is the result of a body of world-renowned investment research collectively known as *modern portfolio theory,* which was first developed in 1952 by Harry Markowitz, a graduate student at the University of Chicago. Markowitz believed that investors are, by nature, risk-averse: When asked to choose between assets that provide the same return potential, investors will select the asset with the lowest risk. In order to accept higher risk, investors expect to be compensated with a higher return.

Markowitz therefore set out to blend asset classes in ways that could minimize risk while also enhancing returns. His research revealed that for every level of investment risk, there is a combination of assets that can generate the highest possible rate of return. By focusing on how asset classes could be used in conjunction with one another to deliver an ideal tradeoff between risk and return, Markowitz's theories ushered in a new and unique approach to money management. The risk of a particular stock or other security wasn't especially important—what mattered more was the security's contribution to the overall risk of an entire portfolio.

Thanks to this insight, investors began shifting their focus from analyzing the characteristics of individual securities toward examining the makeup of the whole portfolio and how it could be managed in terms of risk and reward.

The tenets of modern portfolio theory have since become universally accepted by the vast majority of professional investors, and in 1990, Markowitz and the other academics who pioneered modern portfolio theory were awarded the Nobel Prize in economics. It therefore shouldn't surprise you to learn that large investment firms serving investors with billions of dollars in assets (such as pension plans and endowments) use modern portfolio theory to guide their entire investment approach. We believe that individual investors also should use the lessons of modern portfolio theory when building and maintaining their own portfolios.

THE ESSENTIAL BUILDING BLOCKS OF ADVANCED ASSET ALLOCATION

To use modern portfolio theory and advanced asset allocation strategies effectively, you first need to understand a few important characteristics of the various asset classes. There are three characteristics—historical returns, historical risk, and correlation coefficients—that we call the *essential building blocks* of advanced asset allocation. In this section we'll explain each characteristic in detail and how you can combine them to build an appropriate target-asset mix for your own portfolio.

Essential Building Block Number 1: Historical Returns of Major Asset Classes

In order to build a target-asset mix for your portfolio, it's first necessary to understand the types of returns you might reasonably expect from a variety of asset classes. Exhibit 4-2 shows the long-term historical returns of four major domestic asset classes from the end of 1925 through mid-2003: small-cap stocks, large-cap stocks, bonds, and Treasury bills (cash). As you review these returns, some interesting patterns emerge.

Most investors recognize that stocks offer the greatest potential for asset growth. But it may surprise you just how significantly

EXHIBIT 4-2

The big picture—growth of $1 from 1925 to mid-2003. *(Wilshire Associates.)*

MARKET INVESTMENT RETURNS
Growth of $1 invested from year-end 1925 to June 30, 2003

stocks have outperformed other asset classes over the long term. A $1 investment in the Standard & Poor's (S&P) 500 Index of large-company stocks at the end of 1925 would be worth $2659 in mid-2003. The same investment in U.S. small companies would have done even better, growing to $8300. By contrast, $1 invested in U.S. bonds would have grown to $72, and it would have grown to just $19 if it had been invested in 30-day Treasury bills (cash).

Looking abroad, we see that international equities also have delivered strong returns that have handily outpaced fixed-income and cash investments over time. Foreign shares have gained 10.1 percent annually since 1970, the longest time period of data available for this asset class.

The long-term annualized return for six major asset classes is summarized in Exhibit 4-3.

It's important to note that these returns are long-term averages. You should not expect any asset class's return in a single year to match up perfectly with its long-term historical performance. Typically, an asset class's short-term returns are much higher or lower than the norm. Stocks, for example, rarely post calendar-year returns around their long-term annualized return of 10.2 percent (see Exhibit 4-4).

Essential Building Block Number 2: Historical Risk of Major Asset Classes

Based on the historical return data you've just reviewed, it may seem extremely tempting to invest all your money in stocks or even

EXHIBIT 4·3

Historical returns of major asset classes.

Asset Class	Annualized Return, 1926–2002
U.S. small-cap stocks	12.2%
U.S. large-cap stocks	10.2%
International stocks	10.1%*
Long-term government bonds	5.5%
Intermediate-term government bonds	5.4%
Treasury bills (cash)	3.8%

*1970–2002.
Source: Ibbotson Associates.

EXHIBIT 4·4

Feast or famine (performance is calculated assuming reinvestment of all dividends and capital gains on a daily basis). *[Ibbotson Associates (December 31, 1926–December 31, 1970) and Standard & Poor's (January 1, 1971–December 31, 2002).]*

S&P 500 INDEX YEAR-BY-YEAR TOTAL RETURNS FROM 1926–2002
(All values shown in percentages)

<-20%		20%< x <-12%		-12%< x <-8%		-8%< x <0		0< x <8%		8%< x <12%		12%< x <20%		> 20%	
1930	-24.90	1973	-14.69	1929	-8.42	1934	-1.44	1947	5.71	1926	11.62	1944	19.75	1927	37.49
1931	-43.34			1930	-8.19	1939	-0.41	1948	5.50	1959	11.96	1949	18.79	1928	43.61
1937	-35.03			1940	-9.78	1953	-0.99	1956	6.56	1968	11.06	1952	18.37	1933	53.99
1974	-26.47			1941	-11.59	1977	-7.16	1960	0.47	1993	10.08	1964	16.48	1935	47.67
2002	-22.10			1946	-8.07	1981	-4.92	1970	4.01			1965	12.45	1936	33.92
				1957	-10.78	1990	-3.10	1978	6.57			1971	14.30	1938	31.12
				1962	-8.73			1984	6.27			1972	18.99	1942	20.34
				1966	-10.06			1987	5.25			1979	18.61	1943	25.90
				1969	-8.50			1992	7.62			1986	18.67	1945	36.44
				2000	-9.10			1994	1.32			1988	16.61	1950	31.71
				2001	-11.89									1951	24.02
														1954	52.62
														1955	31.56
														1958	43.36
														1961	26.89
														1963	22.80
														1967	23.98
														1975	37.23
														1976	23.93
														1980	32.50
														1982	21.55
														1983	22.56
														1985	31.73
														1989	31.69
														1991	30.47
														1995	37.58
														1996	22.96
														1997	33.36
														1998	28.58
														1999	21.04

The S&P 500 Index has grown at or about its average rate of return of 10.20% only 4 times in 77 years. ────▶

8% < x < 12%	
1926	11.62
1959	11.96
1968	11.06
1993	10.08

one segment of the stock market such as small caps. However, such an approach would be foolish for you to take because it fails to account for one of the most important factors in the investment process—risk.

Higher potential returns go hand in hand with higher volatility. It's because of the risk inherent in stocks relative to fixed-income securities and cash that investors are able to earn higher rates of return in stocks over time. But stocks, as we know, can swing wildly in the short term and expose investors to a high risk of suffering significant losses from time to time in pursuit of those outsized gains.

Unfortunately, simply knowing that stocks generally are more risky than bonds or cash is not enough to build a truly effective portfolio that can maximize your success. Instead, you must determine quantitatively how much risk each asset class carries by using a statistical measurement called *standard deviation*.

Standard deviation indicates how far from the mean (average) an investment's historical performance has been. An asset class's total return each year reasonably can be expected to fall within one standard deviation of its expected rate of return approximately two-thirds of the time. For example, an asset class with a 1-year standard deviation of 6 percent and an expected return of 8 percent should post returns that fall between 14 percent (8 + 6) and 2 percent (8 − 6) about 67 percent of the time.

Exhibit 4-5 shows the standard deviations of five major asset classes. The higher standard deviation of stocks—both domestic and international—relative to bonds and cash means that their returns are more likely to swing dramatically during the short term. This is especially the case with volatile small-company stocks. Their annual return can be expected to range all the way from 45.4 to −21.0 percent about two-thirds of the time.

Despite the considerable short-term volatility associated with a high standard deviation, the severity of the range of returns of stocks diminishes the longer you hold them. Investors who have consistently held large-cap stocks for 15 years or more (starting on the first of the year) have never lost money, whereas small-cap investors have never lost money over any 20-year period (see Exhibit 4-6). This

EXHIBIT 4-5

Historical risk of major asset classes, 1926–2002.

Asset Class (Least Volatile to Most Volatile)	Standard Deviation	Annualized Long-Term Return
Treasury bills (cash)	3.2%	3.8%
Long-term government bonds	9.4%	5.5%
S&P 500	20.5%	10.2%
International stocks	22.6%	10.1%*
U.S. small cap stocks	33.2%	12.2%

*1970–2002.
Source: Ibbotson Associates.

CHAPTER 4

EXHIBIT 4 · 6

Best and worst returns: U.S. stocks (1926–2002).

Asset Class	Best/Worst 1-Year Return	Best/Worst 5-Year Return	Best/Worst 10-Year Return	Best/Worst 15-Year Return	Best/Worst 20-Year Return
U.S. large caps	54%/-43.3%	28.6%/-12.5%	20.1%/-0.9%	18.4%/0.6%	17.9%/3.1%
U.S. small caps	142.9%/-58.0%	45.9%/-27.5%	30.4%/-5.7%	23.3%/-1.3%	21.1%/5.7%

Source: Ibbotson Associates.

is one reason why we focused on your time horizon in the first step of this process. If you intend to invest in stocks for long periods, you can afford the short-term ups and downs that come with equity investing.

The evidence reveals that the range of returns of international stocks also becomes narrower the longer you invest (see Exhibit 4-7). Investors in international stocks have not lost money over any 10-year period since 1970.

The lower standard deviation of long-term government bonds (9.4 percent) means that their returns will fluctuate less from year to year. Despite their relative stability, however, bonds can carry sizable risks. Rising interest rates hurt bond prices, and bonds with long maturities of 20 or 30 years are more affected by rising rates than are short- or intermediate-term issues. As a result, long-term bonds are less likely to add a dose of stability to a portfolio. In the 1950s, for example, long-term Treasury bonds had an annualized return of –0.1 percent. In contrast, intermediate-term bond prices generally are more stable, thanks to their shorter maturities. Intermediate-term bond investors have never lost money over any 5-year period since 1926 (see Exhibit 4-8).

Cash investments offer the lowest volatility, as measured by standard deviation (3.2 percent) and, not surprisingly, the lowest long-term historical annualized return (3.8 percent). While cash equivalents such as Treasury bills and money market accounts are appealing for their stability, they simply cannot provide the growth needed to get you to your goals on time (see Exhibit 4-9).

Essential Building Block Number 3: Correlation Coefficients

You now have a good idea of the types of returns and risk that each asset class under consideration is likely to deliver on its own. Remember, however, that modern portfolio theory seeks to manage the risk and return of an entire portfolio, not just the individual components in it. This means that you must figure out how you'll combine various asset classes in ways that will add the most value to your investment strategy and give you the best possible return for the level of risk with which you are comfortable.

The key is to build a portfolio of asset classes that do not move in lockstep with each other. In this way, a negative return from one asset class in your portfolio can be offset by a positive return from another.

EXHIBIT 4-7

Best and worst returns: International stocks (1970–2002).

Asset Class	Best/Worst 1-Year Return	Best/Worst 5-Year Return	Best/Worst 10-Year Return	Best/Worst 15-Year Return	Best/Worst 20-Year Return
International stocks	69.9%/−23.2%	36.5%/−2.6%	22.8%/4.3%	21.6%/3.4%	16.3%/10.5%

Source: Ibbotson Associates.

EXHIBIT 4-8

Best and worst returns: Bonds (1926–2002).

Asset Class	Best/Worst 1-Year Return	Best/Worst 5-Year Return	Best/Worst 10-Year Return	Best/Worst 15-Year Return	Best/Worst 20-Year Return
Long-term government bonds	40.4%/−9.2%	21.6%/−2.14%	15.6%/−0.1%	13.5%/0.4%	12.1%/0.7%
Intermediate-term government bonds	29.1%/−5.1%	17.0%/1.0%	13.1%/1.3%	11.3%/1.5%	10.0%/1.6%

Source: Ibbotson Associates.

EXHIBIT 4-9

Best and worst returns: Cash (1926–2002).

Asset Class	Best/Worst 1-Year Return	Best/Worst 5-Year Return	Best/Worst 10-Year Return	Best/Worst 15-Year Return	Best/Worst 20-Year Return
Treasury bills (cash)	14.7%/0.0%	11.1%/0.1%	9.2%/0.2%	8.3%/0.2%	7.7%/0.4%

Source: Ibbotson Associates.

Correlation is what you'll use to determine the extent to which different asset classes move with each other. *Correlation* is a mathematical representation of the relationship between asset classes during an investment cycle. If two asset classes have a correlation of +1, they are said to have *perfect positive correlation*, and their values will move simultaneously in the same direction. If the assets have a correlation of –1, they have *perfect negative correlation*. Their prices therefore will move in exactly opposite directions.

By combining asset classes with low correlations, you can put together a portfolio of very volatile assets (those with high standard deviations) while actually reducing your portfolio's overall risk and achieving a smoother ride (see Exhibit 4-10).

Before we show you specific correlation data, a few examples of correlation relationships should be reviewed. To see low correlation at work, consider the performance of stocks and bonds over time shown in Exhibit 4-11. Bonds tend to perform well during periods when stocks are suffering, and vice versa. By combining stocks and bonds into your portfolio, you can achieve strong returns while lowering the portfolio's overall level of risk. This gives you the benefits of diversification.

EXHIBIT 4·10

Correlation. *(AssetMark Investment Services, Inc.)*

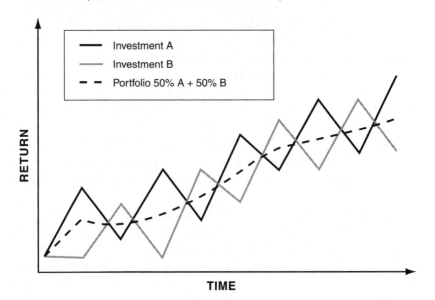

EXHIBIT 4-11

When stocks zig, bonds zag. *(UBS Global Asset Management.)*

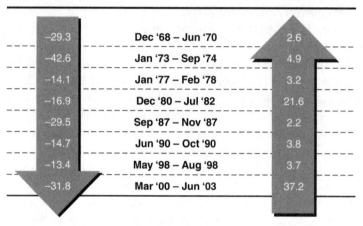

BONDS HAVE DONE COMPARATIVELY WELL WHEN STOCKS HAVE NOT

U.S. Stocks %		U.S. Bonds %
−29.3	Dec '68 – Jun '70	2.6
−42.6	Jan '73 – Sep '74	4.9
−14.1	Jan '77 – Feb '78	3.2
−16.9	Dec '80 – Jul '82	21.6
−29.5	Sep '87 – Nov '87	2.2
−14.7	Jun '90 – Oct '90	3.8
−13.4	May '98 – Aug '98	3.7
−31.8	Mar '00 – Jun '03	37.2

In contrast, you gain little or no diversification benefits if you combine two highly correlated assets with correlation relationships that are equal or close to +1. For example, dividing your money between the S&P 500 and the Dow Jones Industrial Average would not create a well-diversified portfolio. The reason: Both indices are made up of large-cap stocks of U.S. firms, so their prices almost always will move in the same direction—a bad day for the Dow will not likely be offset by a good day for the S&P 500.

The idea here is that advanced asset allocation is not simply concerned with dividing up your assets—it focuses on dividing them up scientifically in intelligent and effective ways. By ignoring correlation, you could easily fall into the trap of dividing your money among two indices—in this case the S&P 500 and the Dow—and still end up with ineffective diversification.

We've listed the correlations of several major asset classes in Exhibit 4-12.

Notice the negative correlation between some of the asset classes, such as long-term government bonds and foreign stocks (as measured by the MSCI EAFE Index). These asset classes therefore will tend to move in opposite directions and provide diversification

EXHIBIT 4·12

Correlation among major asset classes (1970–July 2003).

Asset Class	S&P 500	U.S. Small Caps	Long-Term Government Bond	Treasury Bills	Foreign Stocks (EAFE)
S&P 500	1.0000				
U.S. small caps	0.2615	1.0000			
Long-term government bonds	–0.0287	0.0679	1.0000		
Treasury bills	0.7325	0.1312	–0.0543	1.0000	
Foreign stocks (EAFE)	0.5478	0.1478	–0.0448	0.4328	1.0000

Source: Ibbotson Associates.

benefits if both are included in a portfolio. In contrast, the returns of international stocks follow the S&P 500's returns somewhat closely and will provide a lesser degree of volatility reduction when the two asset classes are combined.

USING THE THREE BUILDING BLOCKS TO SELECT YOUR ASSET CLASSES

Now that you know the essential building blocks of advanced asset allocation, you can move on to the next step: deciding which asset classes you want to include in your own portfolio. You have seen that stocks have delivered the strongest returns of any asset class over time. Therefore, you'll need to include stocks in your portfolio to provide the growth necessary to reach your goals on time and keep well ahead of inflation. Both large- and small-cap stocks should be considered because their returns are not highly correlated. As a result, your portfolio can achieve greater diversification benefits by including both. Likewise, growth stocks and value stocks often move in somewhat different cycles (see Exhibit 4-13). Sometimes growth stocks post positive returns when value stocks are negative. Sometimes both groups deliver negative returns, but to different degrees.

International stocks also play a significant but often overlooked role in building a diversified portfolio. Many U.S. investors tend to favor domestic stocks and therefore miss out on an increasingly large number of opportunities to enhance their returns by investing in

EXHIBIT 4-13

Value and growth stock returns are not closely correlated. *(BARRA.)*

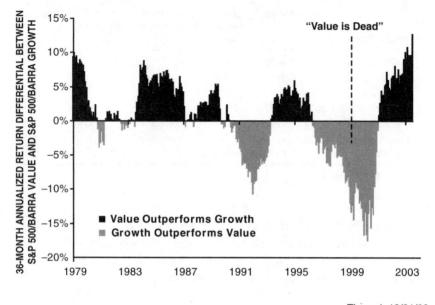

Through 12/31/02

other countries' markets. In fact, the United States now makes up a smaller percentage of the total investable capital market than it did three decades ago (see Exhibit 4-14). International stocks can help to increase portfolio diversification and reduce overall volatility and therefore should be included in most investors' portfolios.

Fixed-income securities, as we've seen, have delivered much lower returns throughout history than stocks and have a harder time keeping ahead of rising prices. However, bonds as an asset class have provided investors with more consistent returns and stability than equities. Meanwhile, cash equivalents such as Treasury bills historically have generated returns even lower than bonds and therefore should represent a small percentage of most portfolios. Typically, cash is used to provide for short-term liquidity needs such as facilitating cash-flow requirements.

BUILDING AN EFFICIENT PORTFOLIO THROUGH OPTIMIZATION

The next step in creating a portfolio using modern portfolio theory is to combine your chosen asset classes in the most effective

EXHIBIT 4-14

Total investable capital market. *(UBS Global Investment Services, Inc.)*

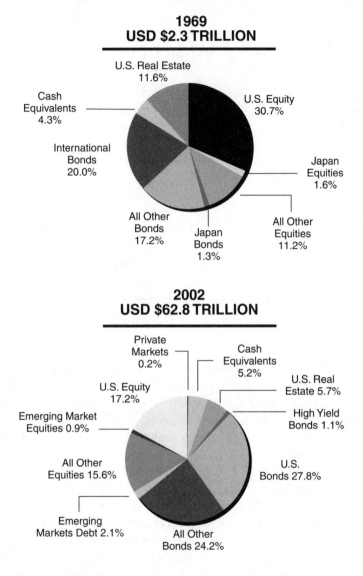

1969
USD $2.3 TRILLION

U.S. Real Estate 11.6%
Cash Equivalents 4.3%
International Bonds 20.0%
All Other Bonds 17.2%
Japan Bonds 1.3%
All Other Equities 11.2%
Japan Equities 1.6%
U.S. Equity 30.7%

2002
USD $62.8 TRILLION

Private Markets 0.2%
Cash Equivalents 5.2%
U.S. Real Estate 5.7%
U.S. Equity 17.2%
High Yield Bonds 1.1%
Emerging Market Equities 0.9%
All Other Equities 15.6%
U.S. Bonds 27.8%
Emerging Markets Debt 2.1%
All Other Bonds 24.2%

way. Through his research, Harry Markowitz discovered that there is an infinite number of ideal combinations of asset classes, each capable of generating the best possible return for a given level of risk. These combinations are known as *efficient portfolios*, and the collection of all these portfolios makes up the *efficient frontier* (see Exhibit 4-15).

EXHIBIT 4-15

The efficient frontier. *(AssetMark Investment Services, Inc.)*

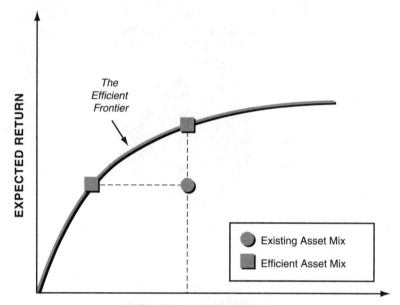

As an investor looking to make the smartest possible decisions with your money, the only portfolios you should consider are those which lie along the efficient frontier. Most of the portfolios that investors choose fall well below the efficient frontier because the combinations of asset classes that investors use in their portfolios offer subpar returns or excessive risk.

As you move forward, compare your own portfolio to an efficient portfolio. Even if you are happy with your portfolio's return over time, you will find that an alternative asset mix—one that is efficient—will give you the same return with less risk. If you are happy with the level of risk in your portfolio, you will see that an efficient portfolio can generate a higher return at that same level of risk.

What's more, research indicates that the more asset classes you include when building an efficient portfolio, the more opportunities you have to enhance performance without taking on more risk (see Exhibit 4-16).

So how do you combine asset classes in a way that ensures that your portfolio is an efficient one? Thanks to advanced computer programming now widely available, an answer can be calcu-

CHAPTER 4

EXHIBIT 4·16

The more asset classes, the better (asset allocation efficient frontier includes both U.S. and foreign stocks). *(Wilshire Associates.)*

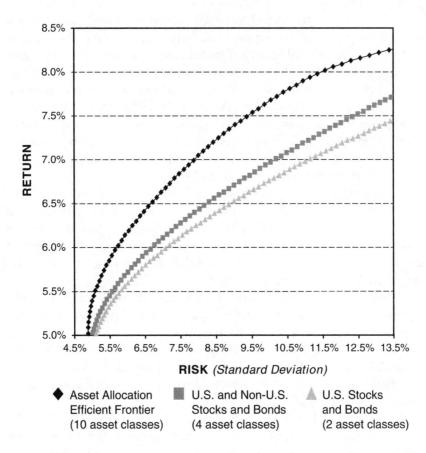

RISK *(Standard Deviation)*

◆ Asset Allocation
Efficient Frontier
(10 asset classes)

▪ U.S. and Non-U.S.
Stocks and Bonds
(4 asset classes)

▲ U.S. Stocks
and Bonds
(2 asset classes)

lated mathematically using portfolio-optimization software, also called *optimizers.*

Optimizers, which were unavailable to individual investors prior to the advent of microtechnology, are capable of figuring the combinations of asset classes that constitute an efficient frontier. Each point on the efficient frontier generated by an optimizer by definition represents a portfolio that provides the highest potential return for the level of risk it incurs. Your optimal portfolio from among all those choices will be one that strikes an acceptable balance between risk and return based on your goals and tolerance for short-term volatility.

On the one hand, using an optimizer is easy. By inputting the three building blocks of advanced asset allocation—the historical returns, risk, and correlation of your chosen asset classes—the software will create an efficient frontier. However, using an optimizer in a way that truly adds value to you as an investor is a much greater challenge.

The reason: Advanced asset allocation is as much an art as it is a science. The process requires you to go beyond simply looking at history and make intelligent judgments about several crucial factors. One of these factors that we've discussed previously is the choice of asset classes you decide to include and exclude from your portfolio. And because financial markets are dynamic, there are frequent changes in the various asset classes' returns and risk, as well as the correlation relationships between them. For example, international stocks have shown a higher correlation to U.S. stocks over the last few years than they did a few decades ago.

Your optimization process therefore also must include estimates about asset classes' *future* returns, risk, and correlation. In short, portfolio optimization is only as good as the assumptions that go into it—and a great deal of consideration must be taken to use this technology to its full potential. As the famous computer axiom says: Garbage in, garbage out.

Two sets of assumptions in particular require much thought because of their dramatic effects on a portfolio optimizer's results. The first is capital markets assumptions—essentially predictions about the financial markets' performance over the next 1 to 3 years. Minor changes in the expected return of an asset class that are inputted into an optimizer can alter the recommended asset allocation significantly (see Exhibit 4-17).

In Exhibit 4-17, portfolio B is an optimal portfolio based on the historical data (return, risk, and covariance) from 1979 to 1998. The inputs for portfolios D and E are the same as for portfolio B except that the expected mean return for the S&P 500 is increased and decreased by 1 percent, respectively. Portfolios F and G are based on historical data from 1926 through 1998, except that the expected mean return for 1-year government bonds is increased and decreased by 1 percent, respectively.

Notice how these slight adjustments lead to dramatically different asset allocation recommendations. For example, a 1 percent reduction in 1-year government bonds' expected return significantly boosts the recommended allocation to stocks while also introducing an asset class—intermediate-term government bonds—not even present in the other portfolios.

EXHIBIT 4-17

Sensitivity of optimizer to inputs.

				Percentage of Portfolio in Each Asset Class		
Portfolio	Inputs Used	S&P 500	Ibbotson Small Stocks	Ibbotson Intermediate-Term Government Bonds	Ibbotson 1-Year Government Bonds	Treasury Bills
B	1979–1998	20.11%	0.00%	0.00%	42.10%	37.79%
D	Increasing S&P 500 expected return by mean 1%	19.54%	0.00%	0.00%	31.72%	48.75%
E	Decreasing S&P 500 expected return by mean 1%	20.5%	0.00%	0.00%	54.43%	25.00%
F	Increasing 1-year government bonds expected return by mean 1%	14.14%	0.00%	0.00%	53.56%	32.39%
G	Decreasing 1-year government bonds expected return by mean 1%	23.52%	0.00%	5.03%	0.00%	71.45%

Source: Richard D. Glass, Stan Marshall, "Portfolio Optimizers: The Road to Financial Security or the Primrose Path?", *Personal Finances and Worker Productivity,* June 1999, Volume 3, Number 1, Virginia Polytechnic Institute and State University.

The second set of assumptions that must be weighed carefully involves the constraints you put on your chosen asset classes. When using optimization technology, limitations must be placed on the percentage that each particular asset class will represent in your portfolio. Otherwise, an optimizer will automatically recommend a portfolio consisting entirely of the best-performing asset class.

For example, an unconstrained optimizer used by an investor who's willing to include small-company stock in his or her portfolio would generate a recommendation that the investor allocate 100 percent of his or her assets to the small-cap sector. The reason: Small-cap stocks have outperformed other major asset classes over time, so the optimizer gravitates toward the asset class with the best long-term rate of return.

Of course, an all-equity portfolio—especially one made up entirely of volatile small caps—is unacceptable for all but the most aggressive investors. Therefore, you must decide the maximum amount that each asset class will be allowed to represent in the overall portfolio. Once again, we see that minor differences in constraint decisions will create radically different efficient portfolios. Research shows that a less than 0.25 percentage point adjustment to one asset class among a group of 10 will generate a completely different allocation.

TWO APPROACHES TO BUILDING EFFICIENT PORTFOLIOS

There are two primary ways to build efficient portfolios using advanced asset allocation methodologies. One is *strategic* asset allocation; the other is *tactical* asset allocation. As we explore both, you'll see that they share many traits but also differ significantly in how they identify and maintain efficient portfolios. Neither approach is inherently superior. In fact, investors often incorporate both methods into their investment program. In Chapter 5 we'll help you to decide if one approach is better for you or if a combination of the two makes sense.

Strategic Asset Allocation

The strategic asset allocation approach essentially incorporates the building blocks we explored earlier. It examines historical patterns of behavior (returns, risk, and correlation) among asset classes over very long periods to understand asset-class behavior. These data are used to generate long-term, forward-looking assumptions about the likely behavior of each asset class in a variety of possible economic environments. These assumptions are then used to generate a long-term target mix of assets for a portfolio.

The key characteristic you should remember about strategic asset allocation is that the target mix stays relatively constant over the investment time horizon. This is so because each new year of data about an asset class doesn't significantly alter its long-term pattern. For example, a strategic asset allocation portfolio of 60 percent stocks and 40 percent bonds likely would retain that consistent target mix for several years. This is not to say that a strategic allocator doesn't review the asset-class assumptions and asset mix and implement subtle changes as appropriate. On the contrary, this type of consistent review of constraints, the relationships between asset classes, and other factors is necessary to evaluate the long-term impact of changes in the global markets and economies on the target mix.

At our firm, we currently use the portfolio target mixes shown in Exhibit 4-18, based on six risk/return profiles that serve as guidelines when constructing efficient portfolios for our clients.

Tactical Asset Allocation

The second method of asset allocation is the tactical method. The tactical decision-making process generally begins with the same steps as strategic asset allocation: Using the principles of modern portfolio theory, a long-term target mix is determined by selecting

EXHIBIT 4-18

Six target-asset mixes. *(AssetMark Investment Services, Inc.)*

Asset-Class Composition	Capital Preservation	Balanced Income	Balanced	Balanced Growth	Growth	Aggressive Growth
U.S. equity	20%	30%	40%	50%	60%	59%
International equity	0%	10%	20%	25%	30%	39%
Fixed income	78%	58%	38%	23%	8%	0%
Cash	2%	2%	2%	2%	2%	2%

asset classes and processing their return, risk, and correlation characteristics—as well as future assumptions and asset-class selections—using advanced optimization software.

Where tactical asset allocation differs is in how that target-asset mix is managed. Unlike strategic allocation, in which the portfolio's target-asset weightings stay more or less consistent during the entire investment period, tactical allocation establishes permissible ranges for each of the asset classes and seeks to shift the target mix whenever there are market opportunities that potentially can boost overall returns or reduce overall risk.

Tactical asset allocators constantly examine the major asset classes, making judgments about their relative attractiveness and looking for opportunities that exist (at investment firms that use tactical asset allocation, these judgments typically are made by investment policy committees consisting of economists and investment professionals). If stocks look extremely cheap relative to bonds, for example, a tactical strategy may increase a portfolio's stock allocation to the highest permissible percentage. Meanwhile, the allocation to fixed-income securities may be reduced to the lowest allowable percentage.

Setting permissible ranges for each asset class is a crucial element of successful tactical asset allocation. For example, a portfolio's long-term target allocation to stocks may be 50 percent, with a minimum allocation of 30 percent and a maximum of 70 percent. Such defined parameters allow a tactical investor to be flexible enough to exploit opportunities as they arise without going overboard and taking on too much (or too little) exposure to any particular asset class. This is one important way in which tactical asset allocators differ from market timers, who typically shift money entirely out of one asset class (stocks, say) into another (cash) based on their economic and market assessments.

Three Tactical Methods

Tactical asset allocation strategies usually involve three methods of decision making, although some investors tend to emphasize one over the others. The first uses fundamental analysis to determine which asset classes appear overvalued or undervalued relative to their own historical prices or to other asset classes, using well-established metrics such as the price-to-earnings ratio or the price-to-book ratio, dividend yields, and discounted-cash-flow models. Fundamental investors often use these metrics to examine the valuation gap between growth and value stocks, small- and large-cap shares, or U.S. and non-U.S. equities. When the gap looks especially wide by historical standards, these investors may increase their exposure to the undervalued asset category.

This approach creates a disciplined way for investors to consistently buy low and sell high, thereby sidestepping the emotions of the marketplace. One of our investment partners, UBS Global Asset Management, which manages more than $400 billion for its clients, uses a fundamental approach to tactical asset allocation that estimates an asset class's future cash flows and discounts them to determine an intrinsic or "fair" value. If the current market value is roughly 10 percent or more below the estimated fair value—if it's cheap, in other words—UBS will consider increasing its position in that asset class. Once the current market value rises to roughly 10 percent or more above intrinsic value, the position may be reduced.

The second approach is called *technical analysis* and is used to spot trends in the market. This methodology is employed by another of our investment partners, Meeder Asset Management. Meeder examines indicators such as the advance/decline line to evaluate the market's overall strength. If stock market indices are rising, the number of stocks advancing should be higher than the number declining. Sometimes, however, this is not the case—which serves as a warning sign to technical investors who look beyond the obvious. In 1999, for example, Meeder saw that decliners far outweighed advancing issues even as the Nasdaq and S&P 500 soared to ever greater heights. The firm also saw that the number of stocks making new highs during this time was much smaller than those hitting new lows—another indicator that signaled market weakness "behind the scenes." Later that year, Meeder reduced its recommended equity allocation to 50 percent—just months before the market began a 3-year slump.

A third method incorporates the lessons of behavioral finance. Behaviorists examine investor sentiment, bullish/bearish consensus, and other factors to spot market inefficiencies brought on by investors overreacting to well-known data and overlooking other news. For example, some behavioral-influenced tactical strategies find a negative relationship between investor sentiment and the direction of the market. As a result, these tactical investors may reduce their exposure to stocks during periods when Wall Street strategists, investment newsletters, and individual investors are extraordinarily—behaviorists might say *irrationally*—bullish, and vice versa. A firm that we work with, PanAgora Asset Management, uses behavioral characteristics in its tactical approach. PanAgora believes that investor behavior is based largely on Federal Reserve Board policy. When the Fed lowers interest rates, investor confidence increases, and investors begin thinking more long term and don't react strongly to new economic or market data. As a result of this behavior, overall market volatility falls. When the Fed raises rates, fears arise over the prospect of recession. Investors become more short-term oriented and often react severely to any bit of new information.

In Chapter 7 we'll explore how investors use tactical and strategic asset allocation strategies to rebalance their portfolios as changing market conditions affect the target-asset mix.

THE MOST IMPORTANT INVESTMENT DECISION YOU'LL EVER MAKE

Asset allocation is not an investment decision that you can afford to take lightly or approach in a haphazard fashion. As we've seen, it plays a critical role in your success as an investor and clearly requires a great deal of time and attention to get the job done right. The sophisticated tasks involved in advanced asset allocation—such as choosing asset classes; making assumptions about their future performance, risk, and correlation; and developing appropriate constraints—demand that you bring superior levels of skill, discipline, and capabilities to the process. Without them, you will not achieve the full benefits of an efficient portfolio.

For these reasons, many investors enlist financial advisors for assistance with asset allocation. Unfortunately, simply hiring an advisor is not sufficient. Too often we see advisors who focus more on selling products to their clients than on helping them allocate their assets in ways that will deliver the maximum benefits. This is why we caution investors who are working with financial advisors to assess their advisors' asset allocation capabilities carefully (we'll show you how in Chapter 15). As you'll see in Chapter 5, a better approach is to enlist the help of a portfolio strategist that is dedicated to the advanced asset allocation process.

Regardless of whether you choose to work with a professional or go it alone, you owe it to yourself as an intelligent investor and to your family to make the types of high-level, prudent asset allocation decisions that will maximize your probability for success.

The Portfolio Strategist: Your Investment Plan's Coach

A t this point, it's time for the seventh-inning stretch. True, we've only reached Chapter 5, but let's take a minute to focus on a topic that we're sure many of you enjoy more than investing—baseball.

Imagine that you own a professional baseball team. As the owner, you bring the financial resources and set the organization's goals and objectives. Let's assume that you think big: Your goal is to win the national championship every year, and you're willing to do what it takes to bring home a World Series trophy every year. After all, if you're going to own a team, why not aim to be the best?

Your job, of course, is to build a team that has the greatest chance of fulfilling your goal. This means that you (and your general manager) have to find the right coach—someone with the talent to bring together the best players in the league and get the most out of them so that you'll win as many games as possible. Your coach also must be able to adapt his strategy based on the strengths and weaknesses of each specific opponent. For example, a good coach knows to bring in the team's top curve-ball pitcher when facing a lineup of league-leading fastball hitters.

As an investor looking to build your own winning game plan, you're in the same position as a baseball team owner. You bring the money to the table and set the overall tone of the program. Your financial advisor, if you work with one, acts as your general manager by providing you with the information you need to make smart decisions and by reporting the status of your team's development. If you invest independently, of course, you also fill the role of your investment plan's general manager. Either way, the coach that you should be looking for is one who can bring together the best possible players at each position and use them to their full potential in order to maximize your financial success.

In the investment world, that coach is known as a *portfolio strategist*. Just like a baseball coach, a portfolio strategist also chooses the right "players"—in this case the individual asset classes and money managers for your portfolio—and combines them in the optimal way based on your specific situation, goals, return objectives, and risk tolerance. Portfolio strategists are one of the key elements that differentiate good investors from great investors. The largest investors in the world regularly employ portfolio strategists to lead them to victory. This is why we believe that you will increase your chances of becoming a successful investor significantly by incorporating a portfolio strategist into your plan.

WHAT ARE PORTFOLIO STRATEGISTS?

If you're not sure what portfolio strategists are, you're not alone. Until recently, the only investors who had access to portfolio strategists were pension plans and other very large institutions with many millions or even billions of dollars at their disposal. Individuals with smaller sums simply weren't invited to the party. We're happy to report that this situation has begun to change in recent years and that individual investors increasingly are gaining access to the same dedicated professionals that serve the world's biggest and most powerful organizations.

Portfolio strategists are teams of analysts, academics, and other investment experts that typically are part of large institutional investment management operations. The world's most respected financial services firms, such as Goldman Sachs and UBS Global Asset Management, have dedicated teams of portfolio strategists that serve their largest clients. These strategists all share one overarching purpose: to build optimal portfolios managed by the best financial minds in the business.

Portfolio strategists have three main responsibilities that they undertake on behalf of investors:

1. Selecting asset classes in which to invest

2. Determining and maintaining optimal target mixes of those asset classes

3. Selecting and monitoring investment managers

As you can see, portfolio strategists address the key factors that are responsible for portfolio performance. For example, portfolio strategists make the full range of asset allocation decisions that we discussed in Chapter 4—including asset class selection, reviewing the historical characteristics of each asset class, making judgments about their future characteristics, and building efficient portfolios that deliver the maximum potential return at a given level of risk. They also decide on the most appropriate money manager for each asset class by rigorously evaluating hundreds of mutual funds and individual managers. Just as our baseball coach wants to find the best shortstop, the best catcher, and so on, a portfolio strategist seeks to identify the top large-cap growth manager, the top small-cap value manager, etc. (We'll explore how to evaluate managers in Chapter 6.)

If you think that these responsibilities aren't much different from the ones you or your advisor have, you're right. All investors looking to maximize their success must address these three factors. The difference lies in how portfolio strategists make these all-important decisions. Simply put, strategists devote themselves exclusively to these issues. All their efforts are focused on determining optimal asset allocation strategies and identifying and monitoring superior investment managers. As a result, we believe that portfolio strategists offer extraordinary value to investors looking to make the smartest possible decisions about managing their money. We're not the only ones: Leading companies such as Saks Fifth Avenue and Shell Oil, as well as top universities like Cornell, all use portfolio strategists.

Portfolio strategists offer unsurpassed expertise and capabilities in three main areas:

- *Substantial research across global capital markets.* Many portfolio strategists have offices and research professionals throughout the world, giving them unique insights into local markets that would be difficult for most investors to possess. For example, UBS Global Asset Management employs 450 investment analysts in 15 countries to conduct research on asset classes, risk management, and asset allocation strategies.

These global resources allow portfolio strategists to have an extremely detailed and up-to-the-minute understanding of countries' economic conditions, political environments, and industries. This makes portfolio strategists well positioned to identify investment opportunities and to make optimal decisions about how assets should be allocated among various regions, countries, securities, and investment styles the world over.

- *Asset allocation and portfolio strategy as a core competency.* As we saw in Chapter 4, the asset allocation decision-making process requires great care and consideration. Portfolio strategists acutely understand that asset allocation drives performance, and therefore devote enormous resources to studying asset classes and how they interact with each other to make the most accurate constraint and capital markets assumptions. Consider one of our investment partners, Goldman Sachs, which has managed assets for high-net-worth investors and large firms such as General Motors and John Deere since 1969. Goldman Sachs has developed industry-leading asset allocation and risk-management technology known as the *Black-Litterman global asset allocation model* that uses advanced return and correlation forecasting techniques to build portfolios that optimally balance return and risk. Likewise, PanAgora Asset Management uses a system of unique, proprietary investment models that enables it to evaluate the relative attractiveness of stocks, bonds, and other asset classes at various stages of the business and economic cycles.

- *Investment policy committees composed of senior investment professionals who engage in a disciplined investment process.* Advanced technology alone is not sufficient to perform superior asset allocation, of course. Portfolio strategists understand this fact and use investment policy committees (IPCs) to scrutinize and evaluate their recommendations. IPCs are made up of an investment firm's most senior professionals, who typically have several decades of experience managing assets. For example, the members of PanAgora Asset Management's IPC have 21 years of investment experience on average. The members of IPCs are often Chartered Financial Analysts (CFAs) and leading academics from the nation's premier business schools. Consider the IPC at UBS, which includes or has included the authors of the renowned Brinson asset allocation study we showed you in Chapter 4. Likewise, Goldman Sachs' team is lead by Bob Litterman, the codeveloper of the aforementioned Black-Litterman model.

IPCs hold their strategists to the highest standards by ensuring that disciplined investment processes are used consistently. For example, in 1999—a year when investors sank $176.4 billion into stock funds[1]—UBS's committee concluded that the U.S. market was nearly 50 percent over-valued based on its valuation metrics. However, instead of ignoring valuation as so many investors did that year, the firm chose to reduce its equity allocation significantly and eliminate its exposure to technology stocks. The result, as you might guess, is that UBS was able to steer its investors away from much of the carnage that occurred during the ensuing years. They stuck to their convictions because their extensive experience told them that the "new economy" was yet another speculative bubble that was bound to end badly.

The power of an experienced portfolio strategist's disciplined investment philosophy is enormous. By having systems in place to develop efficient portfolios, strategists can reduce portfolio volatility and deliver more consistent returns for investors from year to year. The more consistent your return—that is, the less it fluctuates—the faster your money will grow. For example, say that you're comparing two portfolios that each has an expected return of 10 percent annually. The portfolio with less volatility actually will have a higher compound rate of return and end up with a higher value over time. As you can see in Exhibit 5-1, risk reduction does more than help you sleep better at night—it enables you to build significantly more wealth.

DO YOU REALLY NEED A DEDICATED PORTFOLIO STRATEGIST?

Yes, investors should incorporate professional management at the portfolio strategy level into their own investment plans, just as the world's largest and most successful investors do. This is not to say that investors are incapable of making intelligent decisions when it

EXHIBIT 5-1

Less volatility means more wealth. *(Wilshire Associates.)*

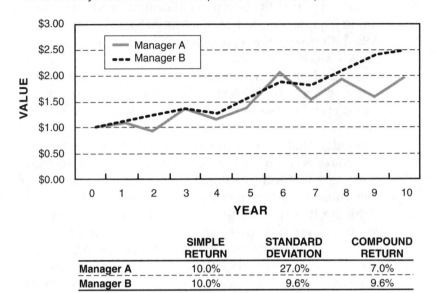

	SIMPLE RETURN	STANDARD DEVIATION	COMPOUND RETURN
Manager A	10.0%	27.0%	7.0%
Manager B	10.0%	9.6%	9.6%

comes to asset allocation and investment management selection. There are plenty of smart, disciplined individuals who do a good job managing their hard-earned savings.

Our stated goal, however, is to help you achieve the maximum level of success—to go from being a good investor to being a great one. You therefore must determine if your own investment program will realize a significant amount of value by using a portfolio strategist. To make an accurate assessment, examine your own level of investment expertise and the amount of research and other resources you can bring to the process. Review the components that go into advanced asset allocation, such as making assumptions about the future performance and correlation of various asset classes, putting constraints on those asset classes, and using optimization technology effectively. Also factor in decisions such as selecting the best managers in each of the asset classes you wish to own and combining them in the most effective way. Think about the amount of time you can reasonably commit to these tasks (and how much time you *want* to commit).

By assessing each of these areas of portfolio strategy, you are in essence asking yourself, "Am I the most qualified person to make these decisions?" You may find that you have the time, training, and temperament to act as your investment plan's portfolio strategist. If not, you may find it advantageous to delegate these duties to the types of professionals who are most capable of consistently making successful choices in these areas.

Selecting a portfolio strategist to make allocation and manager decisions is no different than allowing a mutual fund manager to pick the stocks you own: You're simply tapping the resources of a professional to handle a job that you can't or don't want to do. However, we believe that a portfolio strategist is an even more important resource in your investment plan, given the overwhelming role asset allocation plays in your eventual success. Increasingly, we see investors opting to seek help in this area. Consider that 90 percent of affluent investors indicate a desire to work with financial advisors.[2] What's more, asset allocation is the main investment decision where investors want help (see Exhibit 5-2).

However, we believe so strongly in the value of a dedicated portfolio strategist that we don't recommend that investors delegate asset allocation and management selection decisions to a financial advisor or stockbroker. Most advisors have the best intentions of serving their clients well. Even great advisors, however, often lack the time or the resources to make superior portfolio strategy decisions. Advisors must spend a great deal of their time responding to clients' questions and concerns, as well as running their own businesses, leaving them little time to devote to advanced asset allocation techniques or manager evaluation.

PORTFOLIO STRATEGIST SELECTION

It is imperative to find a portfolio strategist whose approach and methods match your own beliefs about investment management

EXHIBIT 5-2

Services the affluent want from advisors.

	Percent Wanting the Service
Asset allocation	56.7%
Financial/estate planning	41.2%
Tax planning	23.5%
All others	4.3%

Source: Russ Alan Prince and Karen Maru File, *Cultivating the Affluent* (Institutional Investor, Inc., New York).

and risk. If not, you may be uncomfortable with the strategist's choices. You also are more likely to doubt the decisions that are made, especially during periods when a particular strategist's approach temporarily falls out of favor. This could prompt you to switch investment styles or chase after hot market sectors at exactly the wrong time.

The important thing to remember is that you want to work with a strategist whose approach is philosophically and practically in line with your own investment profile. This means that you'll want to decide on factors such as

- *Strategic versus tactical.* As you learned in Chapter 4, there are two methods of asset allocation. Strategic asset allocation sets long-term target-asset mixes that stay relatively consistent over time. This essentially is a passive investment approach used often by investors who are willing to accept returns that are in line with the broader market. Tactical asset allocation, by contrast, sets wide target ranges for the asset classes and over- or underweights them based on the opportunities in the current market environment. If tactical investors see exceptional growth potential or good value in U.S. stocks relative to other asset classes such as overseas equities or bonds, for example, they might increase their portfolios' exposure to stocks while reducing their stake in bonds and foreign markets. Tactical allocation is employed commonly by investors looking to take advantage of areas of the market that they think offer the best opportunities at a particular moment. These investors believe that superior managers can beat their benchmarks by actively exploiting short-term inefficiencies.

- *One strategist versus multiple strategists.* No two investors' philosophies and goals are exactly the same, so it's unreasonable to think that every investor will benefit to the same degree from one investment approach. Achieving the right combination of strategists can help you to better customize your investment plan to meet your goals.

  Using more than one strategist carries several benefits. Because allocation styles go in and out of favor from time to time, using multiple strategists that take fundamentally different approaches to asset allocation can reduce your overall risk. For example, strategic or passive allocation often delivers superior performance during bull markets, when stocks as a group tend to rise. Conversely, tactical asset allocation tends to do best in bear markets, when there may be more rotation in leadership by various asset classes or when opportunities are sparse. By combining the two approaches, temporary poor performance from a strategic strategist may be offset by relatively strong results from a tactical strategist. Strategic allocation also can be used to reduce the risk of an all-tactical portfolio, which depends more on making decisions about the short-term results of asset classes and markets.

- *Standard or tax-managed portfolio.* If you're investing through an individual retirement account (IRA) or other qualified plan, a tax-managed strategy is not required. However, affluent investors in high marginal tax brackets investing in regular accounts might consider strategists who pay close attention to minimizing tax liabilities. There are a number of methods that strategists can use to reduce investors' tax burden, such as selecting managers who buy stocks with low dividend payouts, trade infrequently, or regularly offset capital gains with capital losses. Conversely, tax-sensitive fixed-income portfolios may consist largely of tax-exempt municipal bonds instead of taxable securities. Also, investors concerned about taxes might favor a strategic asset allocation approach, which typically involves less portfolio adjustments than tactical allocation.

- *Domestic versus global.* As we saw in Chapter 4, roughly half the world's investment opportunities are found outside the United States. Therefore, we believe that investors give themselves the best chance of achieving better returns and greater diversification by investing globally.

We believe that asset allocation's importance in the investment process means that it should be addressed with great care and extremely capable resources. Some individual investors will find that they feel comfortable acting as their own strategists, whereas others will identify financial advisors with the focus and capacity to do a superior job. Most investors, however, are likely to be best served and maximize their chance of success by taking advantage of the full range of benefits offered by dedicated portfolio strategists.

NOTES

1. Investment Company Institute, 2003.
2. Merrill Lynch Investment Managers, 2001.

CHAPTER

Implementing Your Plan

Once you've crafted an intelligent asset allocation strategy, your next step is to implement your plan by selecting specific investment vehicles. These choices require a careful assessment of the most appropriate types of managers and investments that will allow you to implement your desired strategy in the most efficient and effective way.

As you now know, asset allocation is a significant determinant of your portfolio's performance. This means that the mutual funds or other investments that you choose must consistently stay within their target-asset classes in order for your allocation strategy to work. To see why this is so important, consider a very simple example. Say that you want to invest 60 percent of your assets in U.S. stocks and 40 percent in government bonds, so you buy one fund that invests in stocks and another that invests in bonds. But what happens if the manager of your stock fund decides to shift some assets into government bonds? In that case, your exposure to bonds may be significantly higher than your plan calls for. Likewise, small-cap fund managers may start drifting into shares of medium-sized or even large companies as assets in their funds grow and they are forced to look beyond their stated asset class for investment ideas. As you'll see later, such shifts can derail your carefully crafted asset allocation plan.

THE RIGHT INVESTMENT VEHICLE FOR YOU

The first step in implementation is to determine which types of investment vehicles are best given your specific situation. You should choose only those types of investments which enable you to build a portfolio with the proper amount of diversification you require based on your allocation decisions.

The most appropriate investments will depend primarily on the amount of your investable resources. When we work with clients who have less than $1 million in assets, we strongly recommend that they use investment vehicles such as mutual funds, variable annuities, exchange-traded funds (ETFs), or a combination of all three. These options typically have low minimum investment requirements of $5000 or less, and as a result, they allow investors with relatively modest sums to gain access to the full range of asset classes that they need to achieve a level of diversification that strikes the optimal balance between risk and return. Investors with $100,000, for example, would have no difficulty building a portfolio of funds representing all the major asset categories—including large- and small-cap U.S. and overseas stocks, value and growth and various bond market sectors, as well as alternative investments such as real estate. The low minimums and flexibility associated with these three investment vehicles, all of which we'll discuss in later chapters, allow the vast majority of investors to construct and maintain the types of portfolios that are well suited to provide winning investment results.

Another type of investment that has grown in popularity during recent years is a privately managed account. Investors using this option hire their own private money manager from a large institutional investment management firm. Privately managed accounts offer many attractive benefits (see Chapter 11). For example, you own all the securities in such an account and therefore can influence what's bought and sold (with a mutual fund, by contrast, those decisions are often made at the fund level by the manager). However, we believe that private accounts are not the most appropriate choice for investors with less than $1 million in investable assets. Minimums on these accounts are typically quite high, at around $100,000 per individual manager, which prevents investors with modest sums from achieving the level of asset class diversification they need. For example, an investor with $500,000 typically could build a portfolio of just five asset classes and would be forced to ignore the rest. What's more, that investor would have to weight all five types of assets equally instead of having the ability to, say, emphasize large-cap value shares.

Unfortunately, many brokerage firms today are aggressively selling privately managed accounts to clients with only a few hundred thousand dollars or less to invest. These firms are often playing to the desire of investors to have an investment that's exclusive and fun to talk about with friends or business associates. As an investor looking to make the most intelligent choices possible, we urge you to consider the effects on your overall diversification before making the decision to use privately managed accounts—or any type of investment. Although it's tempting to have your own money manager running the show, you should never allow an investment vehicle to overshadow your unique asset allocation strategy.

PASSIVE OR ACTIVE: WHAT'S YOUR APPROACH?

Your second decision when implementing your plan is to decide if you'll take a passive or active approach. Passive investing, or indexing, has become an enormously popular way for investors to implement their plans, and its benefits are well established. By trying to match the performance of a specific target index, a passive investor does not actively buy and sell securities in an attempt to beat the market. Instead, the investor holds all (or a representative sample) of the index's securities. The benefits of indexing include:

- *Low expenses.* Management fees on index funds are lower than those on actively managed funds. Index funds also make fewer trades, helping to keep costs down.
- *Predictability.* You typically can count on an index fund to deliver a return roughly in line with the index it tracks.
- *Tax efficiency.* Infrequent trading also means that index funds generally distribute fewer taxable capital gains than most actively managed funds.

Investors using advanced asset allocation also like index funds for their transparency—that is, it's very easy to know all the specific holdings in a fund that tracks an index simply by reviewing the securities in that index. What's more, index funds remain consistently invested in a particular asset class (a Standard & Poor's 500 Index fund won't ever buy high-yield bonds). This makes the important job of maintaining your intended exposure to various asset classes quite easy using an indexed approach.

Investors who favor a passive investment style also might consider ETFs as their implementation vehicle. ETFs invest in a wide variety of indices (some very broad and some very tailored to one small sector), offer consistent asset allocation, and carry even lower expenses than most index mutual funds. In Chapter 10 we'll provide a detailed discussion of ETFs that will help you to decide if these investments are appropriate for your situation.

That said, many investors prefer to hold at least some, if not all, of their assets in investments that are actively managed. The goal of an actively managed fund is to outperform (over the long term) a specific market index such as the Standard & Poor's 500 Index or the Russell 2000 Index of small-cap stocks. Whereas an index fund should deliver a return roughly in line with its benchmark, actively managed investments offer the potential for higher returns if the manager can identify securities or asset classes that will outperform others. Active managers also have the flexibility to reduce overall portfolio risk by deemphasizing investments that they believe to be overvalued. The potential to enhance returns and effectively manage risk has made active management strategies a popular option among pension plans and other large investors with billions of dollars in assets.

However, active management presents several challenges—especially if you're trying to build and maintain an optimal portfolio. For example, how can you know if the manager running an actively managed fund will make investment decisions that are in line with your own approach to asset allocation and risk? Active managers don't specifically track an index, and as noted earlier, their allocation policies can conflict with investors' planned strategies. Furthermore, studies have shown that most active managers—as many as 75 percent, according to some figures—fail to beat their benchmarks in any given year due to such factors as high trading costs and expenses, as well as poor investment decisions. The upshot: You can benefit greatly from an active approach—but to do so, you must identify those select managers capable of

- Consistently beating their indices
- Maintaining a consistent investment style

Make no mistake: Identifying active managers who possess these two crucial characteristics is not an easy task—but it can be done. In fact, the types of investors we encourage you to emulate are adept at building actively managed portfolios run by index-beating managers who stick to their respective investment styles. They are able to identify those managers who consistently deliver value to investors year after year, because they use the right tools and ask the right questions.

THE MORNINGSTAR MYTH AND OTHER TRAPS

Before we show you how these world-class investors identify great money managers, let's look at how investors typically choose their managers. One common approach is to use the fund ranking system developed by Morningstar, the well-known mutual fund research company that tracks more than 14,000 funds. Morningstar assigns funds a star rating based on such factors as return and risk. One star is the lowest possible rating, whereas five stars is the highest.

Morningstar's analysis offers important insights into a fund's investment methodology, historical performance and risk, specific holdings, and other data. However, many investors attempt to take shortcuts by buying those funds which have garnered four- and five-star ratings, naively assuming that the funds that have earned Morningstar's highest honors are the best in existence. Think about your own investing experiences: Have you ever selected a fund entirely or largely because Morningstar had given it four or five stars?

The evidence we've seen strongly suggests that star rankings have an oversized effect on investors' decisions whether or not to invest in a fund. A 2001 study by the Federal Reserve Bank of Atlanta examined how changes in Morningstar ratings influenced fund cash flows. The study, which covered approximately 3400 stock funds and more than 12,000 rating changes, found that the initiation of a five-star rating on a new fund (one with a 3-year record) results in an average inflow of new money during the next 6 months that is 53 percent greater than the normal inflow. What's more, an upgrade from four to five stars on an older fund increases the rate of inflow into the fund by 35 percent on average during the next 6 months.

Clearly, the influence of ratings changes is enormous—investors pay close attention to the stars and place a high value on their ability to predict a fund's future performance. The big question that you therefore must ask yourself is: "Does chasing after highly rated funds work?"

Once again, much research has been conducted to answer this very question, and the answer appears to be a resounding, "No." Consider these findings from various studies:

- Less than half of all mutual funds rated four or five stars at the beginning of 1998 maintained their high rating by the end of that year (see Exhibit 6-1). Most reverted back to a three-star (average) rating.[1]
- Five-star equity funds returned 106 percent, on average, from 1993 through 2000, compared with a 222 percent total return for the Wilshire 5000, an index representing the broad stock market. Those highly rated funds not only underperformed the market significantly, but they also took on 26 percent more risk (as measured by standard deviation) than the market.[2]
- Amazingly, two- and three-star funds outperformed their four- and five-star peers during the period from 1995 through September 30, 1998. The authors of this study concluded, "the linkage between past performance and future realizations is tenuous if not nonexistent."

Even investors who don't get caught up in the star rankings can find it difficult to identify active managers capable of delivering superior returns over long periods. For example, some

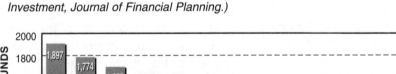

EXHIBIT 6-1

Four- and five-star funds lose their luster. *(TIAA-CREF Institute, Chilton Investment, Journal of Financial Planning.)*

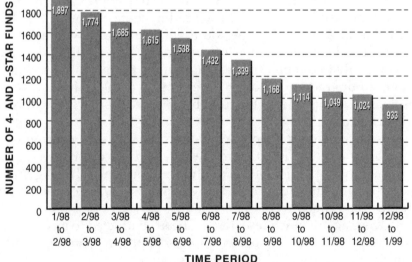

investors examine a fund's performance relative to its peers over long periods, such as the past 5 years. If a manager can deliver exceptional performance over such a time horizon, they think, it's relatively safe to assume that the manager can continue the fund's winning ways going forward.

Unfortunately, we find that a manager's performance over 5-year periods has almost no bearing on future results. A study by Wilshire Associates, one of our investment partners, identified managers from a variety of categories who delivered top-quartile (top 25 percent) returns during the 5-year period from 1992 through 1997. The study then tracked the performance of these managers during the following 5 years (1998 through 2002). The results, compiled in Exhibit 6-2, show that the vast majority of top-performing managers during the first 5-year period failed to stay on top during the next 5-year period.

In particular, notice the small-cap growth category: A meager 7 percent of top-quartile managers from 1992 through 1997 stayed in the top quartile from 1998 through 2002. A full 61 percent of them fell to the bottom quartile. A similar pattern of underperformance is seen in most other fund categories as well.

A BETTER WAY TO SELECT SUPERIOR MANAGERS

If traditional methods of finding superior active managers typically fail, we need to identify a way that truly does work. The very best

EXHIBIT 6·2

Top managers rarely stay on top (first-quartile performance defined as 5-year performance in the top 25 percent of the manager peer group in each asset class, as defined by Wilshire Associates). *(Wilshire Associates.)*

Performance Ranking of 1992–1997 First Quartile Managers Over Subsequent Five Years (1997 through 2002)

Asset Class

	1st	2nd	3rd	4th
Large-Cap Value	14%	28%	25%	33%
Large-Cap Growth	11%	40%	20%	29%
Small-Cap Value	35%	20%	0%	45%
Small-Cap Growth	7%	13%	19%	61%
Fixed Income	30%	8%	19%	43%
International Equity	36%	18%	21%	25%

processes we've discovered through our years of experience are those used by leading investment firms, such as Frank Russell and Wilshire Associates, that serve sophisticated institutions. To show you how we recommend management selection should be done, we'll focus on Wilshire's manager evaluation model. Wilshire Associates is one of the nation's leading institutional investment consulting and technology firms. With over $1.5 trillion in assets under advisement, the firm provides investment advice to such organizations as the California Public Employees Retirement System (CalPERS), Eastman Kodak, Siemens Corporation, and the Commonwealth of Massachusetts.

Wilshire's evaluation model is one of the most highly regarded selection disciplines in the industry. It emphasizes factors that help to identify strong future investment performance, and incorporates both quantitative and qualitative analyses to identify superior portfolio managers. The firm's approach will provide the guidelines you need to effectively choose the types of managers that will help to ensure your investment success.

In particular, Wilshire pays close attention to qualitative or subjective factors because the firm is acutely aware of the fact that past performance largely fails to predict future returns. Wilshire's qualitative process therefore seeks to evaluate managers and management firms by examining such characteristics as

- *Quality of the investment process and philosophy.* Superior active money managers always will have a clear vision of what they are trying to accomplish—an investment philosophy— and a thoughtful, proven process for executing effectively on that vision. One way to find these managers is to determine if they invest systematically in intelligent ways that other investors do not. One example of this is found among managers who use fundamental, research-based methods to invest in small-company stocks. These managers, who recognize that Wall Street typically covers large, well-known companies and often fails to pay much attention to many smaller firms, profit by using a consistent process to find opportunities that are "below the radar" of the vast majority of investors. By contrast, weaker managers tend to invest in simplistic, even naive ways—for example, by basing their investment decisions exclusively on low price-earnings (P/E) ratios or high dividend yields. This type of approach may work sometimes, but it is not advanced enough to systematically deliver index-beating results and add value over time.

- *Experience and talent of investment personnel.* The true assets of an investment organization are the ones that go up and down the elevators every day—the people. Therefore, it's crucial to assess the experience and talent of the entire organization and determine if they're truly incentivized to deliver great results for investors. This assessment occurs through constant communication with the full range of key members of a firm—from the chief executive officer (CEO) and portfolio managers to analysts and client service personnel. This evaluation is similar to the way world-class analysts size up a company by talking to management, customers, and competitors. In particular, it's important to take note of the firm's compensation structure to determine the priority that the firm places on investing. For example, some senior portfolio managers are paid largely based on rising asset levels at their companies. In some cases, this compensation structure means that managers need to spend a significant amount of time on business development instead of what you're paying them to do—manage your money to the best of their ability.

  Certainly, a manager's experience plays a key role in this stage of analysis. There are no definitive rules about just how experienced a manager should be to earn your trust—even the most seasoned managers will underperform some of the time. However, there's much to be said for management firms with experience throughout many decades and that have navigated successfully through multiple market cycles. Another important factor is the quality of the team supporting the manager. A "deep bench" of analysts and other researchers often leads to a more thorough, research-driven investment approach that generates strong returns over long periods.

- *Stability of the organization.* Even superior managers can have a difficult time doing their jobs if their firms are in chaos. For example, high turnover of employees can be a troubling indicator that the firm is not keeping its people happy. Sometimes when firms are bought by competitors, the culture and dynamics of how people interact with each other change, creating high turnover. By contrast, stable organizations typically are able to implement their investment strategies in the most effective manner because their culture and their personnel tend to be consistent. That said, change is not a bad sign if the company can manage it skillfully. The managers at some extremely large investment companies often rotate from one fund to another or move on to open their own firms. However, these "big money" managers often have scores of extremely talented, experienced analysts who can step in easily with no degradation in the investment approach.

- *Sophistication of portfolio construction and risk management.* All active managers make bets—they emphasize or deemphasize asset classes, sectors, or specific investments based on their investment approach. When evaluating managers, it's imperative to determine if they actually understand the bets they're taking and have rational frameworks for constructing their portfolios that reflect their understanding. If a manager overweights a particular stock relative to the fund's benchmark index, for example, how has he or she arrived at that decision and does he or she understand how it could affect the probability that the fund will under- or outperform the index?

Additional insights can be gained by using quantitative manager assessment tools. One approach is to examine the specific investment holdings in a portfolio to determine if the manager is actually managing the assets according to the fund's stated investment style—or if he or she is engaging in *style drift.*

Style drift occurs when a fund shifts from a specific investment strategy, asset class, or index to another. These shifts can cause your overall portfolio to become unbalanced and alter its entire risk and return characteristics in ways that conflict with your strategy. If your value manager begins chasing after growth stocks when those shares are in vogue, for example, you may find that your portfolio is more exposed to growth-oriented investments than you're comfortable with. When growth stocks fall, the value of your investments could decline significantly. What's more, your value manager who shifted styles most likely will not be well positioned to fully capture the upturn when value stocks rotate back into favor. Not only did you take on excessive risk—your returns suffered as well.

Using a process known as *holdings-based analysis,* investors can analyze the characteristics of each stock in a manager's portfolio in terms of market capitalization (large, mid, or small) and investment style (growth or value) and classify the fund into the appropriate category—large-cap growth, small-cap value, and so on. This process provides investors with a snapshot of the manager's current portfolio that can be compared with past and future snapshots to determine if the investment style has remained consistent or if it's wandered across market capitalizations and investment approaches.

It's also possible to use statistical measures to determine if a manager's past performance is a result of skillful stock picking or just luck. A tool called the *information ratio* compares the excess returns over the benchmark that an active manager delivers for investors over time to the risk that is taken to generate those returns. This is done by dividing the alpha (or excess return) by the standard deviation of that return (known as the *tracking error*). The information ratio therefore focuses on the return and risk that come from a manager's decisions to, say, overweight or underweight particular stocks in the portfolio relative to the index. A higher information ratio suggests that a manager has added significant value for the risk assumed and therefore possesses a greater degree of skill over managers with lower information ratios.

IMPLEMENTATION IS ONLY THE BEGINNING

By now you have a strong understanding of what it takes to turn your plan into a real portfolio populated with the right investments and superior managers. However, your job isn't over once you've implemented your plan. The financial markets change rapidly—and the changes will have an enormous impact on your portfolio. You need to watch both your investments and the professionals managing them on your behalf in order to keep your plan on track. In Chapter 7 you'll see how a disciplined, thorough monitoring process will help to ensure your success over the long term.

NOTES

1. Mark J. Warshawsky, Mary DiCarlantonio, TIAA-CREF Institute, and Lisa Mullan, Chilton Investment, "The Persistence of Morningstar Ratings." *Journal of Financial Planning,* 13, no. 9 (2000) 110–126.
2. John Bogle, "The Stock Market Universe—Stars, Comets, and the Sun," speech before the Financial Analysts of Philadelphia, February 15, 2001.

Staying in Balance

*E*very year, tens of millions of Americans go on diets. When we first start, we're excited and enthused at the prospect of shedding those unwanted pounds that have built up over the years. We might start eating smaller portions or replacing that chocolate croissant each morning with fruit or a health shake. We feel empowered and motivated to do what it takes to succeed.

For many dieters, however, that motivation breaks down over time. A few months go by, and we often find ourselves falling back into old habits and forgetting about the goals we set for ourselves. Gradually, that healthy breakfast is pushed aside and the croissant returns. Somewhere along the way we lose the enthusiasm and discipline with which we started, and our diets once again become imbalanced.

As an investor, you face the same types of challenges on the path to financial success as dieters do when they attempt to lose weight. Think about your own experiences buying stocks, bonds, or mutual funds. Typically, you start out excited by the idea of building a winning portfolio that will get you to your goals on time. You might spend hours, days, or even weeks doing research on markets, asset classes, managers, and specific investments so that you can construct just the right portfolio for your needs. Along the way you consult financial publications, the Internet, family and friends, financial advisors, and other sources.

But what happens a few months down the road? If you're like most investors, your time and attention become refocused on all the other concerns of daily life. Those monthly portfolio statements that you initially ripped open when they arrived in the mail now get pushed to the back of the drawer or filed away and never looked at again. That once strong drive for investment success fades.

Ignoring your investment plan can have serious financial consequences, however. In this chapter we'll show you why it's essential to stay on top of your investments and how to make the right moves to maintain a portfolio that will maximize your chance for success.

MONITORING AND REBALANCING YOUR ASSETS

Your job as an investor isn't over after you've built your portfolio. You can't expect your portfolio to remain static for the simple reason that the financial markets don't stay static—they're in a constant state of flux.

As you saw in Chapter 4, the asset classes in which you've invested won't move in lockstep with each other. This means that the percentage of your assets that you have invested in each category will fluctuate as market conditions change. The target-asset allocation that you chose therefore will drift: As stock prices rise, for example, your exposure to stocks will increase, and vice versa. Depending on market fluctuations, your allocation to stocks over time eventually will become higher or lower than you want it to be. As a result, you may find that you've incurred a higher level of investment risk than you feel comfortable with.

To stay on track, you must rebalance your portfolio's holdings from time to time. Rebalancing provides several benefits that will help you to become a more successful investor. Rebalancing will

- Keep risk in check
- Enhance your overall wealth
- Enable you to systematically "buy low and sell high," removing emotion from your decision making

To see how rebalancing works, consider this simple example: Say that you have $500,000 to invest and want a long-term target-asset mix of 50 percent stocks and 50 percent bonds. You'd therefore hold $250,000 in equities and the same amount in fixed-income securities. If over the next year your stock investments gain 10 percent and your bond holdings rise 5 percent, you'll have a $537,500 portfolio (your stocks would be worth $275,000 and your bonds $262,500). To regain your desired 50/50 percent mix, you'd sell $6250 in stocks and reallocate the money to bonds.

This type of rebalancing is called *strategic asset allocation rebalancing* because asset exposure is readjusted to your target-asset mix at regular intervals (see Exhibit 7-1). Strategic rebalancing should be done each quarter, which studies have shown provides investors with approximately 90 percent of the benefits attainable from rebalancing.

HOW REBALANCING ADDS VALUE

By rebalancing, you continually manage risk and return in accordance with the parameters you spelled out during the discovery process and put down in writing in your Investment Policy Statement. Your rebalancing decisions are designed to prevent you from being overexposed to overpriced areas of the market and to ensure that you're not underexposed to asset classes that are attractively valued and offer greater potential for price appreciation. In short, it's a system that provides a disciplined, unemotional way to consistently take advantage of one of the best investment strategies of all—buy low and sell high.

We can clearly see the benefits of regularly rebalancing back to your intended target mix if we review the market bubble of the late 1990s. As large-company growth stocks and technology shares posted enormous gains year after year, an investor using a disciplined program of rebalancing would have sold stocks from those two categories each quarter and reinvested the

EXHIBIT 7-1

Strategic asset allocation rebalance. *(AssetMark Investment Services, Inc.)*

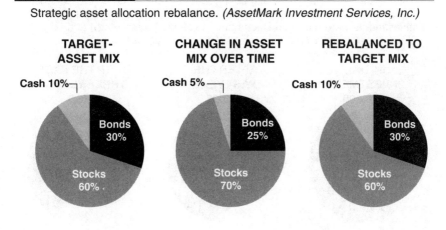

proceeds in bonds to maintain the appropriate mix. By regularly reducing exposure to hot market segments, such an investor would have avoided some of the most painful losses that occurred when large-cap and tech stocks plummeted. And by maintaining the portfolio's exposure to bonds, the investor would have been in a better position than most to benefit when bonds began their extended period of outperformance in 2000.

Numerous academic and investment studies have shown us the benefits of instituting a disciplined rebalancing strategy. Exhibit 7-2 reveals how a hypothetical investor who started with a 60/40 percent mix of stocks and bonds in 1999 ended up over various time periods during the 3 years through 2002. Notice how skewed this investor's portfolio became by not rebalancing. The intended mix has, in fact, been turned upside down: Bonds after 3 years represented almost 60 percent of the investor's assets, whereas stocks had fallen to around 40 percent. Now take a look at your own portfolio during that time. If you didn't rebalance, your allocation mix likely followed a similar path.

Over time, neglecting to rebalance your portfolio can result in an asset mix that creates significantly higher volatility than you ever intended and are comfortable with. And as we have learned, too much volatility can lead you to make rash decisions—such as selling out of stocks entirely—that will damage your carefully crafted investment plan. Exhibit 7-3 shows just how much more downside risk can occur in a portfolio that isn't rebalanced regu-

EXHIBIT 7-2

The dangers of failing to rebalance. [Figures are based on an investment in the Standard & Poor's 500 Index and the Lehman Bond Aggregate Index. Investments were made on December 31, 1999 (3-year return) and on December 31, 2001 (1-year return).] *(Lipper Analytical.)*

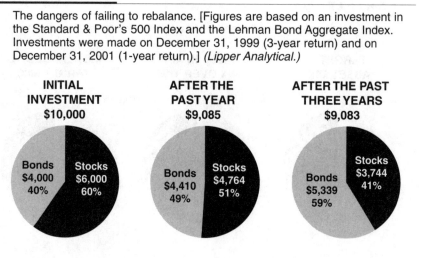

INITIAL INVESTMENT $10,000	AFTER THE PAST YEAR $9,085	AFTER THE PAST THREE YEARS $9,083
Bonds $4,000 40% / Stocks $6,000 60%	Bonds $4,410 49% / Stocks $4,764 51%	Bonds $5,339 59% / Stocks $3,744 41%

CHAPTER 7

EXHIBIT 7-3

Rebalancing can help to lower volatility. (Example is based on a hypothetical portfolio consisting of 60 percent Standard & Poor's 500 Index and 40 Percent Lehman Treasury Index. The portfolio was rebalanced annually every June during the 20-year period. Maximum loss is based on any rolling 12-month period during the 20-year period.) *(UBS Global Asset Management.)*

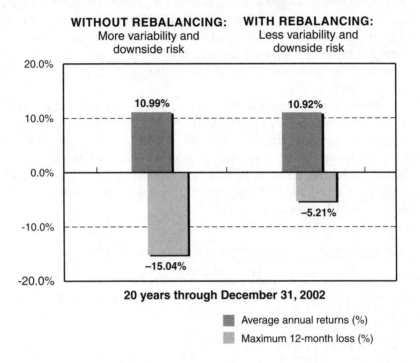

WITHOUT REBALANCING:
More variability and
downside risk

WITH REBALANCING:
Less variability and
downside risk

10.99%   10.92%

−5.21%

−15.04%

20 years through December 31, 2002

■ Average annual returns (%)
▨ Maximum 12-month loss (%)

larly. Notice that the two hypothetical portfolios generate virtually the same return over time. However, the rebalanced portfolio's maximum loss over a 12-month period is significantly less than that of the portfolio that remains static. Let's face it: You're much more likely to stick with your plan if you lost 5 percent during a year than you would if you faced a 15 percent decline.

The volatility reduction that rebalancing provides is important for reasons other than helping you to sleep better at night and stay on track, however. Lower volatility means that your money doesn't have to work as hard to regain ground lost during periods when the markets deliver poor performance. For example, say that your portfolio worth $100,000 plummets by 50 percent during a bear market to $50,000. In order for you simply to break even and bring your portfolio's value back to $100,000, you would need a 100 percent return.

One of our investment partners, Meeder Financial, calls this the "mathematical catch-up game." For every percentage point in investment capital you lose, it takes more than that in a gain to get back to even. The catch-up game is a lot easier to play if you use a disciplined rebalancing strategy. For example, you'd only need an 11 percent return to get back to where you started if your portfolio was less volatile and fell just 10 percent during a bear market (see Exhibit 7-4). Clearly, then, investors who consistently rebalanced during the late 1990s' bull market now have a lot less ground to make up than investors who let themselves get overexposed to the riskiest asset classes.

And as we learned in Chapter 5, lower volatility also carries another important benefit: It actually can help to enhance your overall investment returns over time (see Exhibit 7-5, which shows the growth of $100,000 in two portfolios with different levels of risk). As a result, you can build more wealth by managing volatility through rebalancing than you will by taking a simplistic, static, buy-and-hold approach.

THE BENEFITS OF TACTICAL REBALANCING

Successful portfolio rebalancing also can be achieved by using a tactical approach. Tactical rebalancing, as you might assume, does

EXHIBIT 7·4

The mathematical catch-up game. *(Meeder Financial.)*

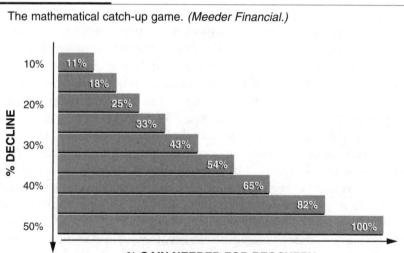

% GAIN NEEDED FOR RECOVERY

EXHIBIT 7-5

Less volatility = greater wealth. *(CEG Worldwide, LLC.)*

Year	Consistent Investment		Volatile Investment	
	Rate of Return	Ending Value	Rate of Return	Ending Value
1	8.0%	$108,000	30.0%	$130,000
2	8.0%	$116,640	−20.0%	$104,000
3	8.0%	$125,971	25.0%	$130,000
4	8.0%	$136,049	−20.0%	$104,000
5	8.0%	$146,933	25.0%	$130,000
Arithmetic return	40.0%		40.0%	
Compound return	8.0%		5.4%	

not seek to rebalance back to a target mix at regular intervals. Instead, a tactical investor constantly monitors the global financial markets and makes rebalancing decisions based on perceived opportunities and risks among various asset classes and market sectors as they arise. As a result, tactical rebalancing can occur at any time.

For example, if stocks look attractive, a tactical investor will increase his or her portfolio's exposure to stocks above its target mix. When stocks appear to be overvalued, by contrast, the allocation will be reduced below the target. On average, however, even a tactical portfolio's allocation will remain fairly close to the target over the course of an entire market cycle (see Exhibit 7-6).

Tactical rebalancing, as you can see, is also based on the idea that intelligent investing requires a systematic way to consistently buy low and sell high. Because tactical rebalancing can involve a higher degree of analysis and forecasting than does strategic rebalancing, investors often find tactical strategies to be more difficult. However, tactical approaches can add tremendous value and should not be overlooked simply because strategic rebalancing is a more straightforward process.

To see the value of a tactical approach, consider the following examples of investors who have consistently delivered strong returns over time using tactical rebalancing:

- In October 1990, the markets were suffering amid a weak economy and high unemployment. Large-cap stocks were

EXHIBIT 7·6

Tactical asset allocation rebalance. *(AssetMark Investment Services, Inc.)*

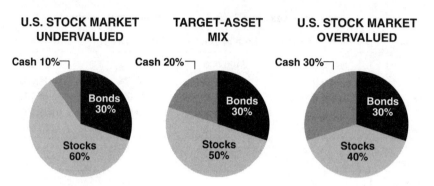

U.S. STOCK MARKET UNDERVALUED	TARGET-ASSET MIX	U.S. STOCK MARKET OVERVALUED
Cash 10%	Cash 20%	Cash 30%
Bonds 30%	Bonds 30%	Bonds 30%
Stocks 60%	Stocks 50%	Stocks 40%

down 12 percent over the previous 12 months, whereas small-cap stocks (–27 percent), high-yield bonds (–13 percent), and REITs (Real Estate Investment Trusts) (–29 percent) fared worse. Investment firm Litman/Gregory Asset Management reallocated assets into these four sectors, each of which gained more than 30 percent over the following year. The result: Litman/Gregory outperformed the market in 1991. Later, in 2000, the firm saw excessive risk in large-cap stocks and instead favored REITs and small-cap value shares. The firm's stock portfolios that year gained 5.1 percent on average, versus an 11 percent loss for the U.S. market overall.

• Investors expected 2003 to begin with a roaring start, citing low valuations and a steadying economy. However, concerns about war with Iraq coupled with poor economic data sent stocks lower. Investment management firm Breen Financial maintained an equity exposure below its long-term target mix and favored growth and large-cap stocks over value and small-cap stocks based on its market analysis. The result: Breen's portfolio gained 1.6 percent during the 12 months through April 2003, compared with a –4.6 percent return for its benchmark.

MAKE REBALANCING A PRIORITY

Clearly, the benefits of rebalancing your portfolio either through strategic or tactical means are compelling. Yet, in our experience, we find that most individual investors fail to rebalance regularly—or at all, in many cases.

Why? For starters, rebalancing requires investors to sell assets that have performed well recently and buy those which have experienced poor performance. As we saw in Chapter 2, selling your winners and buying your losers are extremely difficult decisions to make from an emotional standpoint: They conflict directly with our psychological predisposition to let winners ride and avoid "weak" investments. If every investor approached asset allocation and rebalancing on a purely rational basis, no one would ever find their portfolios overloaded with tech stocks, bonds, company stock, or any other type of asset.

The difficulty involved in regularly selling winners and buying losers is one reason why we have recommended that you incorporate an Investment Policy Statement (IPS) into your financial plan, just as large companies and endowments do when they invest their assets. Your IPS will clearly spell out the rebalancing guidelines you'll follow and therefore will serve as a constant reminder of the actions you know you must take to achieve investment success. Furthermore, by instituting a formal rebalancing policy, you'll remove emotion from your decision-making process and be more comfortable with the types of decisions that aren't always easy to make.

Your IPS also will help to build discipline into your rebalancing process. There's no question that we're busy people with responsibilities to our jobs, our families, and others. The day-to-day concerns we must address make it easy to ignore our portfolios until something—usually a market meltdown or other financial shock—causes us to fret about our investment holdings. Of course, by that time it's usually too late to sidestep much of the damage that occurs. By using an IPS, you'll always be aware of the commitment you've made to your financial future and be motivated to follow through on the smart decisions you made when implementing your plan.

For many investors, there's another stumbling block that prevents them from instituting a rebalancing program—cost. Traditionally, stockbrokers and advisors charged investors for every transaction—every buy and sell—they made. This transaction-based approach often discouraged investors from rebalancing because each trade meant more money investors had to hand over in the form of loads and commissions. Many investors, rightfully so, were suspicious about who was benefiting more from portfolio rebalancing—themselves or their brokers.

Today, thankfully, many options exist that enable you to better control the costs associated with rebalancing. If you invest through a single family of no-load mutual funds, for example, you typically can switch among funds for little or no cost. Also, the rise of fee-based financial advisors gives investors a way to rebalance at lower costs than in the past. Fee-based advisors are paid not by how many transactions clients make but by earning a percentage of the total assets in their portfolios. Many advisors these days also have implemented asset-based pricing, in which a virtually unlimited number of trades can be made for one price. For example, 25 basis points (0.25 percent) may cover all trades over the course of an entire year. By removing the transactional fee structure, these advisors have made rebalancing a less costly and therefore easier step for many investors to take.

MONITORING YOUR MANAGERS

The criteria used for selecting active managers discussed in Chapter 6—such as the information ratio and the stability of the management firm, among others—must be revisited regularly to ensure that your managers are continuing to add value and that the components that have generated their success up to now remain firmly in place. If you invest with passive managers through index funds, you'll also want to make sure that the managers are delivering the returns of the specific indices they are attempting to replicate.

One effective method of monitoring your managers is examining their performance every quarter and looking for significant under- or over-performance relative to the appropriate benchmark. Investors often care a great deal when their managers perform significantly worse than their target index but fail to pay much attention when significant outperformance is delivered. However, both scenarios should be examined closely because large returns to the upside and downside can indicate that style drift may be at work.

For example, let's say that your large-cap value fund trounced the competition and the Standard & Poor's 500/BARRA Value Index during the most recent quarter. By examining the specific sectors and stocks the manager emphasized and deemphasized, you can effectively deconstruct that excess return. You may find that the manager stayed true to a large-cap value discipline and outperformed by selecting superior value stocks or by investing a relatively large amount of assets in specific stocks that posted big gains. Likewise, a holdings-based analysis might reveal that the manager avoided investments that blew up.

Conversely, you might discover that the best performers in the portfolio weren't value stocks at all but instead were growth-oriented shares in which the manager invested to beef up returns. This type of behavior occurred frequently during the late 1990s: As growth stocks soared and value shares remained in a deep funk, some value managers became so-called closet growth investors by buying technology stocks. Such style drift can expose you to significantly greater risk and must be managed.

Manager changes at a fund are also worth noting. Often the manager who has been responsible for delivering excess returns leaves to join another firm or start a new asset-management company. The question you must answer by using the qualitative analysis tools profiled in Chapter 6 is whether or not the new manager is likely to continue delivering strong returns going forward. One good indicator is if there is a deep pool of talent, such as industry analysts, that has worked on the fund in the past and will remain in place.

Be aware that performing this high level of due diligence on your investment managers is a time-consuming endeavor. However, it must be done to ensure that the parameters you've set for yourself are being maintained in all areas of the investment process. It's quite easy and tempting to assume that a manager has your best interests at heart and is consistently doing all that's possible to deliver strong returns at an acceptable level of risk. But truly disciplined investors who view their managers with a healthy amount of skepticism are much more likely to spot the occasional anomalies that occur and be better positioned to evaluate their effect on an overall portfolio.

Assessing Your Progress

*E*very quarter, we recommend that you revisit the goals and strategies you set out with at the beginning of your journey toward financial success. The reason: You need to determine if you're still on track or if any changes need to be made to reflect new developments in the markets or your own unique personal situation.

This process of reporting your investment results and sizing up your progress is a crucial step in the ongoing management of your portfolio. For starters, quarterly reporting enables you to essentially "keep score" of where you are. Are you making progress toward the goals you set for yourself during the discovery process and wrote down in your Investment Policy Statement (IPS)? Is the amount of progress you're making sufficient and in line with your intended risk and return parameters? Do you need to make alterations based on any important changes in your life or on performance-related issues from your investments and managers?

Reporting also gives you the cold, hard facts about your portfolio's performance that are needed to help you to consistently make disciplined, unemotional decisions about your investments. During periods of intense market volatility or poor performance, for example, the headlines in financial magazines and the business sections of newspapers become increasingly alarmist—"Sell Stocks Now!" is one great example we've seen. In a fearful environment in which the media is intent on selling more magazines by playing on your fears, it's easy to become overwhelmed with uncertainty and make rash moves with your money. By engaging in quarterly reporting, you can effectively combat those forces by examining your performance rationally and objectively. The result: Any moves you do make with your portfolio will be based on facts and careful judgments—not the latest scary story you read at the newsstand.

Conducting true reporting that delivers real value to your investment process isn't always easily done, however. Often, the performance documents you receive from brokerage houses, fund companies, and other financial services firms don't supply much of the information that's needed to truly assess your situation and make better decisions about your portfolio.

Consider the monthly statements that arrive in your mailbox. These reports generally provide a snapshot of your portfolio at a particular moment in the recent past by listing your current holdings, recent transactions, and performance during the previous month and perhaps year to date. While such information is useful, it is all that many financial institutions provide—and it simply does not go far enough.

A better approach is to sit down and take the time to put together a quarterly report analyzing the performance of both your overall portfolio and its various components—such as the asset classes and managers selected—relative to the unique strategy and goals that you have established previously. This performance analysis goes beyond a monthly snapshot to include returns over the previous quarter and year, as well as longer periods such as 5 and 10 years and performance since the inception of the portfolio. This detailed level of reporting will allow you to ascertain your performance in relationship to your long-term objectives and assess your progress during multiple time periods. The result, of course, is a significantly clearer picture of your financial situation and how it has evolved, as well as the need for any changes you should make.

THE FOUR STEPS IN REPORTING

Following the end of each quarter—that is, March 31, June 30, September 30, and December 31—you should perform an assessment of where you are versus where you want to be by following these four steps:

Step 1: Note Any Changes to Your Personal or Financial Situation

Significant life changes can alter your goals or financial status, resulting in a shift in the risk/return profile you've identified for

CHAPTER 8

yourself. Therefore, begin your assessment process by listing any major new developments that have occurred in your life during the past 3 months, as well as any that are on the horizon and approaching rapidly. Examples of significant life changes commonly include medical needs for yourself or family members, receiving an inheritance, retirement, and education expenses.

Step 2: Review Your Performance

The key is to review and assess your performance accurately by using the appropriate benchmarks. It's a common mistake to compare the returns of a diversified portfolio of stocks, bonds, cash, and any other asset classes against the performance of a single benchmark that represents only one type of asset, such as the Standard & Poor's (S&P) 500 Index of large-company stocks. By its very nature, a diversified portfolio's returns always will be above or below those of a single asset class. This is why it's crucial to compare your performance against a benchmark that accurately represents the composition of your portfolio.

This is done by creating a composite index of the asset classes you hold, weighted in the same way they're weighted in your own portfolio. As an example, the model portfolios we use represent various mixes of the following widely recognized and accepted benchmark indices: the Wilshire 5000 Total Market Index (the broadest U.S. equity index, representing more than 5700 publicly traded domestic stocks), the Lehman Brothers Intermediate Aggregate Bond Index (which tracks the performance of investment-grade government, corporate, asset-backed, and mortgage-backed bonds), and the Morgan Stanley Capital International EAFE Index (representing the performance of the developed markets outside North America—Europe, Australasia, and the Far East).

Once you've compared your portfolio's performance against the appropriate target benchmark, you must evaluate that performance to determine if it's acceptable. It's at this stage that the facts you generate through reporting can help you to better assess your performance relative to your goals and avoid making poor decisions during turbulent times.

To gauge your performance against your stated goals, you need only compare your portfolio's rate of return over various periods with the desired or expected return you calculated during your initial discovery process and wrote down in your IPS. If you determined that you need an 8 percent annual return to reach your goals on time and your annualized return over the past 5 years or longer is 8 percent or higher, you are clearly on track. Keep in mind, of course, that your rate of return over shorter periods will most likely be higher or lower than your required return over time due to the often-volatile nature of the financial markets during the short term.

It's also important to compare the *expected* returns for your portfolio over short and long time periods against your *actual* returns. This will give you the appropriate context to determine if your plan is still on track. For example, you may be surprised during times when your portfolio posts what look to be excessive returns to the upside or the downside. Such outsized returns may cause you to make rash moves, such as loading up on a hot asset class or dumping one that's cold. By reviewing expected returns based on long-term historical return data, however, you may find that those seemingly abnormal results are actually in line with history.

Consider a hypothetical balanced portfolio consisting of 40 percent U.S. stocks, 20 percent international stocks, 38 percent fixed-income securities, and 2 percent cash. As Exhibit 8-1 shows, such a portfolio can experience significant swings in value, especially over extremely short periods. The worst 3-month return from 1973 through 2002, for example, was −14.5 percent, whereas the worst 6-month return was −20.3 percent. The question that investors with this or a similar type of balanced portfolio need to ask themselves when evaluating performance is: "How do my returns compare with the returns I should reasonably expect to earn based on the composition of my portfolio?"

If, for example, your balanced portfolio fell 12 percent during a quarter, you might be tempted to make a shift in your asset allocation

EXHIBIT 8·1

Range of returns for a balanced portfolio.

Best/Worst 3-Month Return	Best/Worst 6-Month Return	Best/Worst 1-Year Return	Best/Worst 5-Year Return	Best/Worst 10-Year Return
17.6%/−14.5%	29.4%/−20.3%	44.0%/−27.2%	25.7%/1.56%	17.0%/7.4%

Note: This information has been compiled by AssetMark Investment Services, Inc., to reflect the historical returns from January 1, 1973, through December 31, 2002, of the following combinations of indices used to construct the balanced portfolio: 40 percent Wilshire 5000, 20 percent MSCI EAFE, 38 percent Lehman Brothers Aggregate Bond, and 2 percent cash. Returns in excess of 1 year are annualized. There is no guarantee that the objective return of any profile will be achieved. Past performance is no guarantee of future results. Investors cannot invest directly in an index.

Source: AssetMark Investment Services, Inc., December 2002.

strategy. However, by knowing that a –12 percent return is in line with historical returns and does not violate what you should reasonably expect your portfolio to earn during a single 3-month period, you will be more willing to hang on through a particularly rough patch.

Step 3: Account for Your Performance

Ideally, your performance analysis will reveal that your plan continues to be well positioned to get you to your goals on time. But what if you find that your returns are failing to meet your expectations or falling below the acceptable range of returns based on historical performance? In that case, you need to "look under the hood" of your portfolio to assess which components aren't performing at their peak.

Start by examining your asset allocation decisions. Is your portfolio heavily weighted to an asset class that performed poorly during the most recent quarter or several quarters? As we've seen, stocks can be extremely volatile during short periods. If your long-term strategy calls for emphasizing stocks, your portfolio occasionally may suffer extreme short-term underperformance when the stock market experiences a shock such as the Russian debt crisis of 1998 or the technology blowup of the past few years. Likewise, a tactical asset allocation shift to a particular area of the equity market may explain your portfolio's performance. If you've emphasized value stocks over growth shares and value has lagged recently, your returns will reflect that environment.

Next, evaluate the managers you've selected to run your money using the tools we described in Chapter 7. How did each manager's performance compare with the returns of the appropriate index? Also compare your managers' returns with those of their peer groups, as measured by Lipper, a leading source for mutual fund performance data. For example, how has your large-cap growth manager performed relative to the Lipper Large-Cap Growth universe of funds? Conducting this analysis for each of your managers will reveal which ones have performed in line with or beaten their peers and which ones have underperformed. If you do identify a manager who has underperformed during a recent quarter, examine his or her performance over previous quarters and longer periods to determine if the weak returns are an anomaly (even great managers slip up sometimes) or part of a larger pattern of underperformance.

Your assessment also should take into account the recent environment in the financial markets, which you can compile through research reports and market commentary. This information helps to explain portfolio performance by providing details about the most important forces that affected your investments during the quarter—including gross domestic product (GDP) growth, consumer confidence, employment data, and other factors. Conversely, if you work with an advisor, you should expect such quarterly insights into market conditions.

Step 4: Make Any Changes, if Necessary

We strongly believe that patience is a crucial characteristic of successful investing. Therefore, it's important not to get caught up in or overemphasize performance results over short periods such as one quarter or one year. That said, there are times when it's necessary and beneficial to make adjustments to your portfolio that reflect changing conditions.

For example, as a child gets closer to attending college and the need to pay tuition bills approaches, the level of short-term risk you're willing to accept in your portfolio may fall dramatically. You must be certain you'll have enough money on hand to start funding education needs, and as a result, you may decide to shift some assets into investments such as bonds and cash that offer relative stability and liquidity. Likewise, a promotion, job loss, or other change in your employment situation may mean that you now have more (or less) money to regularly contribute to your investment plan. If you have significantly more money to invest going forward, for example, you may need to earn a smaller rate of return on your investments to reach your defined goals on time. As a result, your asset mix may shift: You may decide to more heavily weight lower-return/lower-risk investments. Conversely, you may determine that you want to invest even more aggressively in higher-risk/higher-return investments with the purpose of reaching your objectives earlier.

If you discover that a strategist or investment manager has delivered subpar returns relative to the appropriate benchmark and peer group over a period of 3 to 5 years, you should consider a replacement. Such extended periods of underperformance often indicate that something has changed fundamentally with the investment firm, its management, or the parent company. Here again, we strongly urge you to avoid falling into the trap of buying funds simply because of their strong past performance or high star ratings. It's always best to perform high-level qualitative and quantitative analyses that examine the firm's investment approach, resources, and culture, as well as the manager's investment style and level of skill over time.

 **C H A P T E R**

Picking the Right Funds

*Y*ou could say that investors 20 years ago had it pretty easy. Back then, just 857 mutual funds—which together held $296 billion in assets—existed. Since then, the fund industry has truly exploded, and mutual funds have become a staple of just about every investor's financial diet. Total mutual fund assets now exceed $6 trillion, whereas funds as a percentage of Americans' total household financial assets have soared from 6.7 percent in 1990 to nearly 18 percent today.[1]

Perhaps most tellingly, investors now must choose from more than 8200 mutual funds representing just about every market, country, region, sector, and investment style that exists (see Exhibit 9-1). In short, the mutual fund landscape has become more crowded— and tougher to navigate—than ever.

Due to the proliferation of mutual funds, we find that most investors have become familiar with many of the basic concepts of funds, such as loads and no loads, expenses, and various fund categories. We find that clients who come to see us for the first time often have a working knowledge of mutual funds and often have built portfolios populated with many fund offerings.

Unfortunately, we also find that many investors are still extremely unsure about the choices they have made. Despite all the ink that's been shed over mutual funds, our experience tells us that most investors remain confused about using all that information to build mutual fund portfolios that they feel truly confident are working to their full capacity. Therefore, our goal in this chapter is to show you "what works."

EXHIBIT 9-1

Growth of the mutual funds industry, 1992–2002.

Year	Total Net Assets (trillions of dollars)	Number of Funds	Number of Shareholder Accounts
1992	$1.6	3824	80 million
1993	$2.1	4534	93 million
1994	$2.2	5325	114 million
1995	$2.8	5725	131 million
1996	$3.5	6248	150 million
1997	$4.5	6684	170 million
1998	$5.5	7314	194 million
1999	$6.9	7791	226 million
2000	$7.0	8155	245 million
2001	$7.0	8307	249 million
2002	$6.4	8256	251 million

Source: Investment Company Institute.

The sheer number of articles, Web sites, and books that focus on mutual funds is perhaps one big reason why most investors are constantly spinning their wheels when they try to select funds—or second-guessing their choices after their decisions. The truth is that all the fund information that is thrust in front of us by the media, the Internet, and other sources creates information overload: There's so much out there that processing all of it intelligently becomes a gigantic hurdle over which few investors can leap.

In fact, it's all too easy to get caught up in that information—and misinformation—and make poor choices. Consider the many financial magazines that each year feature headlines screaming, "The Best Funds to Buy for the Next Year." If you follow the advice of these magazines, you set yourself up for failure. For example, *Money* in late 2001 hyped up shares of big technology companies and other so-called glamour stocks as part of the magazine's 2002 forecast. As you are no doubt well aware, technology and other big-cap stocks—and the funds that held them—continued to plummet throughout the following year. The media's fund picks often don't do any better. Consider two of *Smart Money*'s top picks for 2002, AMRO/Veredus Aggressive Growth and Excelsior Energy and Natural Resources. Both funds not only posted big losses that year but also significantly underperformed the average fund in their categories.

We firmly believe that the key to success lies in ignoring the never-ending stream of stories about the right funds to buy at the right time and instead using proven tools and criteria to select those types of funds which give you greater probability of achieving your most important financial goals. Whether you're new to investing and have never purchased fund shares or are an experienced investor with a portfolio stocked with all varieties of funds, you can benefit by understanding the types of mutual funds that will best position your portfolio for consistent, long-term success.

WHY FUNDS?

There's no question that investment vehicles have become more advanced over the years. For example, you can now hire your own money manager through a private account or invest in a hedge fund that at one time wouldn't have let you in the door due to huge minimum investment requirements. This surge in complex investments has caused some investors to look down on "boring" old mutual funds as an antiquated investment of the past.

Although we use a wide variety of investment vehicles at our firm, we believe that mutual funds remain one of the very best options for the vast majority of investors to implement optimal portfolios based on advanced asset allocation techniques. The benefits that exist for fund investors are among the most compelling in the entire investment industry and include

- *Professional management.* Mutual fund managers and their teams of analysts have the full-time job of focusing on the type of research and due diligence that (1) is crucial to selecting superior investments and (2) is too time-consuming and complex for the vast majority of investors to do themselves. By delegating to a professional, you aren't the one who has to pour over financial statements, read numerous industry reports, and interview management, customers, competitors, and the like. What's more, the very best funds are run by the world's top investment firms and individuals—giving you access to some of the brightest and most experienced minds in the investment universe.
- *Diversification.* Funds typically hold a large basket of stocks from a variety of industries, helping to reduce company-specific risk and increase the potential for stronger returns

over time. Funds provide this diversification at a much lower cost than if you tried to build a diversified portfolio of individual stocks. Research has shown that it takes a minimum of 35 individual stocks in each asset class to gain effective diversification benefits. So if you invest in eight asset classes, for example, you'll need to identify—and monitor regularly—at least 280 individual stocks. What's more, building such a portfolio would require an investment of hundreds of thousands of dollars, versus perhaps $50,000 using funds.

• *Flexibility.* By using no-load funds—which don't charge an up-front sales fee for the privilege of investing—you can make changes to your fund portfolios easily and with little to no cost involved. This enables you to rebalance your portfolio or to change managers, if necessary, without having to worry about incurring big expenses.

THE SIX CHARACTERISTICS OF SUPERIOR MUTUAL FUNDS

We've seen repeatedly throughout this book that selecting the best mutual funds for your portfolio can be a daunting task. Clearly, using past performance or star ratings won't get the job done.

So how do we solve the problem? We believe that the most appropriate funds possess a handful of characteristics that enable investors using advanced asset allocation strategies to build the types of optimal portfolios that will get them to their goals on time. If you choose to implement an investment strategy using funds, you'll want to select those funds which stack up well in the following six areas:

Crucial Mutual Fund Characteristic 1: Style-Specific Mandates

We've shown you the negative effects that can occur when money managers "change their stripes" by shifting their investment approach and engaging in style drift. To avoid the problems that result from such actions, you'll need to select funds that remain true to their stated investment philosophies and methodologies—quarter after quarter and year after year. These funds' managers have an unwavering discipline to use research and security selection processes that are focused strictly on a limited universe of investment options from within a given investment style. As a result of using such funds, you effectively retain a high degree of control over your carefully crafted allocation strategy because you don't have to worry about your managers straying from their targets.

Traditionally, it's been somewhat difficult to find funds that maintain style-specific mandates because managers were given much room to roam. The good news is that this situation has begun to change in recent years. Fund companies increasingly are realizing that, given the sheer number of securities in existence, it makes sense for managers to specialize in specific styles and sectors of the market. Specialization allows managers to fully focus on the particular characteristics of an asset class or industry and make more intelligent investment decisions on investors' behalf. That said, style drift remains an all-too-common practice in the industry. As a smart investor looking to make the most intelligent choices possible, you must stay vigilant.

Crucial Mutual Fund Characteristic 2: Multimanager Approach

The vast majority of mutual funds being offered today are managed internally by a single investment firm, with one individual or a small committee responsible for employing the firm's particular investment methodology to make all buy and sell decisions in the portfolio.

We believe that investors are better served by selecting funds that are instead managed by more than one investment firm using multiple managers in the decision-making process. Here's why: If you think about it, no two managers see the world in exactly the same way. Even managers who invest in the same asset class, such as large-cap growth or small-cap value stocks, use a variety of methodologies. Whereas one large-cap growth fund manager will favor stocks with strong earnings momentum or positive earnings surprises and high price-earnings (P/E) multiples, another will focus on growth companies that have temporarily fallen out of favor and trade at relatively low valuations. The result is that although both managers play in the large-cap growth arena, each one's portfolio most likely will look considerably different from the other's.

Clearly, you can see how using more than one manager for a given style can add value. By combining the two types of managers just described, the large-cap growth portion of your portfolio will reflect the best of both worlds: You'll consistently have exposure to the full range of growth-oriented shares of large firms. As a result, you'll have enhanced your portfolio's overall level of diversification and risk management. During periods when momentum stocks suffer, your lower P/E growth holdings (often called *growth at a reasonable price,* or *GARP*) will provide a buffer, and vice versa.

What's more, a multimanager approach frequently generates stronger returns for the amount of risk taken than does relying on a single manager. Consider Exhibit 9-2, which shows the performance of two large-cap growth managers during the 5 years through March 31, 2003. Each manager's returns are strong relative to the benchmark index. However, an investor combining the two approaches would have outperformed the index by a wide margin—and with less risk.

Crucial Mutual Fund Characteristic 3: Portfolio Concentration

Whereas most mutual funds hold 100 to 200 or even more individual securities in their portfolios, concentrated funds are designed to invest in a much smaller number of issues—often as few as 30 to 50 names. The strategy behind concentrated funds is one of the most compelling we've seen in the fund industry. When asked, most fund managers admit that they only have a small number of stocks that they believe are truly superior—their "best ideas" for their portfolios. However, the policies at many investment firms often require these managers to invest in hundreds of companies, with the idea that doing so will increase diversification. In order to stick to these guidelines, the managers must look well beyond their best ideas to second- and third-tier stocks that they use to fill up their portfolios. The result is that the overwhelming majority of investors own "watered-down funds" in which the managers do not have strong convictions about 25 to 50 percent of their portfolios.

Concentrated funds, by contrast, enable managers to place greater emphasis on their very best ideas, giving them the opportunity to show the value of their specific approaches to security selection. When used in conjunction with a multimanager strategy, portfolio concentration can have a powerful effect. For example, two concentrated growth managers using different investment techniques will each populate the fund they share with only the stocks

Benefits of a multimanager approach. *(AssetMark Investment Services, Inc.)*

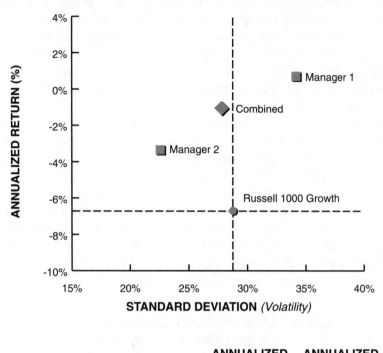

	ANNUALIZED RETURN	ANNUALIZED VOLATILITY
Large-Cap Growth Manager 1	0.85%	34.18%
Large-Cap Growth Manager 2	–3.69%	22.24%
Combined Managers	**–1.09%**	**27.69%**
Russell 1000 Growth Index	–6.72%	28.29%
Annualized Outperformance	**5.63%**	**–0.60%**
Cumulative Outperformance	**31.50%**	

that they feel have the greatest potential for strong growth. That same fund managed by a single, nonconcentrated manager most likely would consist of a few best-idea stocks and a whole lot of also-rans.

A concentrated approach to portfolio management has become one of the most respected approaches to asset management, earning praise from none other than legendary investor and chairman of Berkshire Hathaway, Warren Buffett, who observed that "a policy of portfolio concentration may well decrease risk if it raises, as it should, both the intensity with which an investors thinks about a business and the comfort level he must feel with its economic characteristics before buying into it." Buffet's comment reveals an important element of concentration: Risk reduction can be achieved by holding a smaller—not larger—number of stocks if the manager selecting the stocks does a superior job.[2] Our view is that once you have identified great managers, it makes sense to let those managers focus on the investments they feel most strongly about.

Research by Standard & Poor's shows that a concentrated approach to portfolio management generates superior returns over time. Concentrated funds have outperformed their nonconcentrated peers in nearly every category of domestic equity mutual funds during the 10 years through March 31, 2003 (see Exhibit 9-3). The average 10-year annualized return for concentrated funds of 9.29 percent was roughly 1 percentage point higher than that of nonconcentrated funds, which returned 8.31 percent annually, for all but two style categories (mid-cap value and mid-cap growth). What's more, the typical concentrated fund outperformed the overall category average in almost all categories.

Crucial Mutual Fund Characteristic 4: Tax-Sensitive Management

It's not what you earn; it's what you keep. This is why the world's best investors always keep a close watch on ways to

EXHIBIT 9-3

Concentrated funds outperform.

	Average 10-Year Annualized Return (Category)	Average 10-Year Annualized Return (Concentrated)	Average 10-Year Annualized Return (Nonconcentrated)
Large-cap blend	7.69%	8.14%	7.54%
Large-cap value	8.24%	8.82%	7.86%
Large-cap growth	7.29%	7.52%	7.03%
Mid-cap blend	9.13%	10.06%	8.81%
Mid-cap value	9.13%	8.96%	9.26%
Mid-cap growth	6.96%	5.93%	7.23%
Small-cap blend	10.27%	13.98%	9.90%
Small-cap value	10.13%	11.02%	9.91%
Small-cap growth	7.83%	9.18%	7.27%

Source: Standard & Poor's.

CHAPTER 9

minimize the effects of taxes and keep more money in their own pockets. The types of fund managers we recommend incorporate a variety of approaches aimed at keeping the taxman at bay. One such approach is to sell strong-performing positions only after they've been in the portfolio for at least 12 months, when any gains are taxed at lower rates, and selling weak investments before 12 months' time because short-term losses provide greater tax benefits than do long-term losses. Some managers also focus on tax accounting methods to reduce taxes. The most tax-efficient system, *highest in, first out* (HIFO), sells the highest-cost shares of stock first, thereby generating the smallest possible taxable gain. (*First in, first out*, or FIFO, by contrast, sells the first shares that were purchased. Such shares often have a low cost basis and therefore leave investors with bigger tax bills.)

Crucial Mutual Fund Characteristic 5: Low Expenses

High fund expenses directly affect your bottom line by eating away at a fund's returns. Think about it like this: All other factors being equal, lower costs mean higher returns. Therefore, smart investors only consider mutual funds with no loads and operating expenses (such as management fees) that are lower than average. As you evaluate funds, compare their expenses with the average for their specific categories. Some types of funds carry much higher expenses than others (see Exhibit 9-4).

EXHIBIT 9-4

Average expense ratios (%).

Fund Category	Expense Ratio
Large blend	1.38
Large growth	1.55
Large value	1.42
Mid-cap blend	1.54
Mid-cap growth	1.63
Mid-cap value	1.48
Small blend	1.67
Small growth	1.74
Small value	1.55

Note: Reflects actively managed funds.
Source: Morningstar, Inc.

Crucial Mutual Fund Characteristic 6:
A Best-in-Class Manager

The manager of any mutual fund should meet the selection criteria we detailed in Chapter 6 on investment manager selection. This assessment process can be undertaken by individual investors or delegated to a portfolio strategist.

A WORD ABOUT VARIABLE ANNUITIES

Variable annuities (VAs) are a sort of cousin to traditional mutual funds, in that they enable you to invest in professionally managed portfolios of stocks, bonds, and other asset classes, as well as a variety of styles (such as growth and value). Therefore, the rate of return you earn in a VA will depend largely on the performance of the underlying investments (by contrast, investors in fixed annuities generally receive a guaranteed rate of return over a specific time period).

However, VAs differ from mutual funds in several significant ways. Unlike regular taxable mutual funds, contributions to VAs grow tax-deferred—that is, any gains, dividends, or interest is sheltered from taxes until money is withdrawn from the account (which typically occurs when an investor reaches retirement). This tax deferral often appeals to younger investors saving for retirements that may be decades away. At that point, investors can choose to take a lump-sum payout or annuitize the account and receive regular income payments.

VAs also carry life insurance features that can be used for estate planning—for example, death benefits that a VA's beneficiary receives when the account owner dies. Retirees and older investors often favor VAs for the peace of mind that such insurance features provide for themselves and their heirs.

VAs have a number of features that must be evaluated to determine if they are an appropriate option for implementing your plan. Apart from their ability to provide tax-deferred growth— probably the single most important element—VAs offer several other intriguing benefits:

- *Tax-free switching.* Transferring money between various VA investment options (or subaccounts) does not generate taxes, making them one good option for tactical asset allocation investors looking to consistently emphasize and deemphasize certain areas of the financial markets.

- *Unlimited contributions.* Unlike with individual retirement accounts (IRAs) and other types of retirement vehicles, VA investors can contribute as much money as they like to their accounts.
- *Death benefits are guaranteed.* A beneficiary won't receive less money than the amount invested in a VA (minus any withdrawals), even if the current balance falls below that level. For example, if you invested $100,000 in a VA and the value fell to $90,000, your beneficiary would still receive the full $100,000 if you die before the payout phase. If your VA's value rises above the amount you've contributed, your beneficiary gets the higher amount. What's more, some VAs essentially "lock in" your earnings every few years to ensure that the beneficiary benefits from gains.

That said, VAs also feature some characteristics that make them less appropriate for certain types of investors. For example:

- *Additional expenses.* VAs charge so-called mortality and expense fees in order to provide the insurance benefits. Although these fees often are quite low (around 0.5 percent or less), some VAs' fees are excessive.
- *Tax and other penalties.* Withdraw money from a VA before age 59½ and you'll get hit with a 10 percent tax penalty. Some annuities also charge surrender fees if you cash out during the first few years. Therefore, money that you think you'll need in the short term should not be invested in a VA.
- *Loss of capital gains.* Money withdrawn from a VA is taxed as ordinary income, not capital gains. Investors who remain in very high income tax brackets even in retirement should consider how this tax structure will affect them.

As you read on you'll come across several alternatives to mutual funds and fundlike investments such as VAs. We strongly encourage you to consider the many options available to you when implementing your plan. However, we also want to remind you not to ignore "boring" old mutual funds—which you may very well find to be the best path to long-term investment success.

NOTES

1. Ivestment Company Institute (2003).

2. Because a concentrated portfolio relies more heavily on the skill of the manager than does a diversified portfolio, it can involve more risk if the stocks selected by the manager perform poorly.

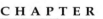

Using Exchange-Traded Funds

*C*hances are you probably hadn't heard of exchange-traded funds just a few years ago, let alone invested in them. In existence since 1993, exchange-traded funds (ETFs) didn't garner much attention from investors until the late 1990s. Since then, however, they've become one of the fastest-growing investment vehicles in history. Total assets in ETFs have grown more than 15-fold since 1997—from $6.7 billion to more than $102 billion by 2003. Likewise, the number of ETFs to choose from has soared from just one in 1993 to 113 today.[1]

Clearly, ETFs have caught on with investors. That said, we find that some of you are confused or intimidated by this relatively new investment. Even investors who own ETFs often tell us that they don't really understand them and how to use them most effectively.

As someone who's looking to make smarter financial decisions, you know that popularity alone isn't a good enough reason to invest in any type of investment vehicle. However, ETFs offer a number of unique features and benefits that make them extremely attractive to many investors. In this chapter we'll take a close look at ETFs—how they work, their pros and cons, and how you can decide if they're the best type of investment vehicle for implementing your investment strategy for success.

THE ABCs OF ETFs

ETFs essentially combine certain characteristics of index mutual funds and individual stocks. For example, ETFs represent a basket of stocks that mirror a particular index, market sector, or asset class, just as index funds do. Like stocks, however, ETFs trade throughout the day on major market exchanges such as the American Stock Exchange (in contrast, fund shares typically trade just once a day).

The first ETF, launched in 1993 by the American Stock Exchange, was the Standard & Poor's (S&P) Depositary Receipts (commonly referred to as SPDRs), which attempts to replicate the performance of the S&P 500 Index of large-cap stocks. Due to the industry's rapid growth, investors can now select ETFs that invest in a full range of broad domestic indices (from the Dow Jones Industrial Average to the S&P Midcap 400), investment styles (such as the Russell 1000 Growth and the Russell 3000 Value indices), specific industries and sectors (energy, health care, financial services, and so on), and foreign markets (from Brazil to Belgium, as well as the broad-based MSCI EAFE). Most recently, bond ETFs have been added to the mix. As a result, investors looking for a passive approach when creating optimal portfolios using advanced asset allocation techniques are now able to use ETFs to meet virtually all their asset class requirements (for a profile of some of the most popular—and most obscure—ETFs currently available, see Exhibit 10-1). And because ETFs mirror market indices, they allow investors to strictly adhere to their target-asset allocation at all times.

ETFs feature an unusual structure that causes them to operate in fundamentally different ways from the typical index mutual fund. The brokerage firm or fund company that sponsors an ETF sells the shares in so-called creation units (blocks of 50,000 shares) to other brokerage firms. Those firms then sell smaller amounts to individual investors, who trade the ETF shares just like they do stocks. The key is that the ETF sponsor never deals directly with the individual investors: You can't sell the shares back to the ETF sponsor and receive cash, as you can with a traditional mutual fund.

Instead, ETF shares being sold are bought by middlemen known as *specialists* or *market makers,* who then deliver the ETF shares to the sponsor and swap them for the underlying stocks that the ETF shares represent (see Exhibit 10-2). This arrangement is called an *in-kind payment* and is considered to be a nontaxable transaction because the ETF itself is not buying or selling stocks in the open market.

EXHIBIT 10-1

The world of ETFs.

Broad-Based ETFs	Ticker
SPDRs (S&P 500)	SPY
Cubes (Nasdaq 100)	QQQ
DIAMONDS (Dow Jones Industrial Average)	DIA
MSCI EAFE Index Fund	EFA
S&P Europe 350 Index Fund	IEV
Style-Based ETFs	
Russell 1000 Growth Index	IWF
Russell 1000 Value Index	IWD
S&P Small Cap 600/BARRA Growth Index Fund	IJT
S&P Small Cap 600/BARRA Value Index Fund	IJS
Sector ETFs	
S&P Global Energy Sector Fund	IXC
Goldman Sachs Technology Index Fund	IGM
Dow Jones U.S. Consumer Cyclical Sector Index Fund	IYC
Country-Specific ETFs	
MSCI Australia Index	EWA
MSCI Japan Index	EWJ
MSCI Sweden Index	EWD
Bond ETFs	
iShares Lehman 1–3 Year Treasury Bond Fund	SHY
iShares GS $ InvesTop Corporate Bond Fund	LQD

Source: AssetMark Investment Services, Inc.

The bottom-line benefit of this seemingly arcane setup for investors is extremely compelling: ETFs are among the most tax-efficient methods of investing currently in existence. Like traditional index funds, ETFs don't trade frequently and therefore tend to distribute taxable gains to shareholders less often than actively managed funds. However, the structure of ETFs also allows them to offer even greater tax efficiency than index funds. Because ETFs trade like stocks, investors never sell shares back to the ETF sponsor.

EXHIBIT 10-2

In-kind ETF transactions. *(Barclays Global Investors.)*

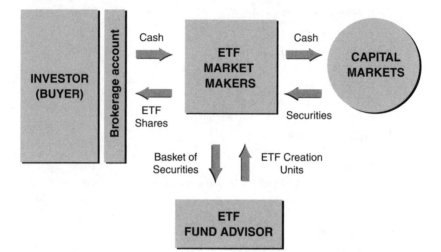

The result: Unlike traditional index funds, ETFs aren't forced to sell securities and incur capital gains to meet shareholder redemptions. ETFs also keep tax liabilities low by determining the specific shares they swap during a sale. When a brokerage firm delivers its SPDR shares back to the sponsor, the sponsor can choose to give back to the brokerage firm the cheapest shares it owns of, say, General Electric. By clearing out these low-cost-basis shares, the ETF further sidesteps potential capital gains.

What's more, ETF investors retain a higher degree of control over their cost basis than do traditional index fund shareholders. Because of the stocklike structure of ETFs, you create your own cost basis when you buy the shares and therefore never enter into a portfolio with "built-in" capital gains. By contrast, you run the risk in an index fund of buying other shareholders' unrealized gains. If, for example, an index mutual fund has unrealized gains (from stocks in the portfolio that have appreciated in value but have not yet been sold) at the time you invest, you'll get hit with a tax bill when those stocks are eventually sold at a profit—even though you weren't around to share in those gains. The upshot: You get taxed on profits from which you never benefited.

ETFs' stocklike structure also translates into lower annual expenses for shareholders (see Exhibit 10-3). Although index funds are widely heralded for their low expenses relative to actively man-

EXHIBIT 10-3

Expense ratio comparisons: active, index, and ETFs.

Fund Category	Average Active Fund	Average Index Fund	Exchange-Traded Fund
U.S. taxable bond	1.08%	0.52%	0.15% (iShares GS $ InvesTop Corporate)
Large blend	1.38%	0.76%	0.09% (iShares S&P 500)
Large value	1.42%	1.19%	0.18% (iShares S&P/BARRA Value)
Small blend	1.67%	0.86%	0.20% (iShares Russell 2000)
Mid-cap blend	1.54%	0.88%	0.20% (iShares S&P 400)
Foreign equity	1.76%	0.99%	0.25% (iShares EAFE)
Sector	1.90%	1.49%	0.60% (iShares DJ)

Source: Barclays Global Investors; Morningstar, Inc.

aged funds, ETFs are even cheaper—often by 50 percent or more. For example, SPDRs charge investors a mere 0.12 percent annually, versus 0.75 percent for the average domestic index fund and 1.53 percent for the average actively managed diversified fund.[2] Because ETF sponsors don't deal directly with individual investors, they don't require the big customer service departments that often add layers of expense at many mutual fund companies. Since higher costs have a direct impact on the real rate of return you earn, ETFs actually enable you to enhance your portfolio's performance year after year and generate a higher compound return that will help you to reach your goals over time.

For investors looking to actively reduce their tax liabilities, ETFs also provide a compelling yet often overlooked advantage. Consider an investor who holds a large-cap growth ETF and a large-cap value ETF that, taken together, represent the stocks contained in the S&P 500. During a period when value stocks fall and growth shares rise, it's possible to sell the large-cap value ETF and take a realized loss, but immediately buy another large-cap value ETF that tracks a slightly different index. An investor in this position remains fully invested in the market and maintains his or her asset allocation strategy while also realizing losses that can later be used to offset any gains.

WHAT TO WATCH OUT FOR

Although ETFs have become increasingly popular and a worthy alternative to index mutual funds, they contain characteristics that may not appeal to some investors. When deciding whether or not to implement your plan using ETFs or a combination of ETFs and other investment vehicles, consider these important factors:

- *Commissions.* You'll usually pay a commission charge each time you purchase ETF shares because your transaction goes through a brokerage firm. This makes ETFs less appealing to investors who like to dollar-cost average by investing small sums each month. For example, say that you invest $100 monthly into ETF shares, paying a $20 commission each time and 0.30 percent in annual expenses. By contrast, your friend puts the same amount each month in an index fund with no commission and an expense ratio of 0.60 percent. Assuming that both investments earn 8 percent annually, you'll end up with $14,485 in 10 years—but your friend will have $17,803.

    Your best bet, therefore, is to use ETFs if you plan on investing large sums of money at one time. Another option is to work only with financial advisors or other investment professionals who use cost-effective asset-based pricing systems, which allow you an unlimited number of trades for a flat annual fee (which sometimes can run as low as 0.10 percent).

- *Pricing.* Unlike mutual funds, whose share prices are equal to the underlying value of the stocks they hold, ETFs' prices rise and fall based on supply and demand (just like stocks). This means that an ETF might trade at a higher price (a premium) or lower price (a discount) than the actual market value of the assets in the fund. Fortunately, this *price gap* is extremely small (often less than 1 percent) among ETFs that track major indices and trade frequently, such as SPDRs and QQQs. The reason: If an ETF trades at a discount, brokerage houses will swoop in and buy the undervalued ETF shares, swap them for the stocks they represent, and then sell those stocks and pocket the difference. The heightened demand for those cheap ETF shares helps to bring their price back in line with the value of the underlying assets.

    That said, ETFs tracking relatively unknown or thinly traded indices can carry significant premiums and discounts. Typically, this occurs with overseas ETFs, such as those which mirror the market of a single country like Taiwan. Part of the reason stems from the fact that the ETF (which trades on a U.S. exchange) and the underlying stocks (which trade in the particular overseas country) aren't trading at the same time, which creates the possibility for inefficiencies that lead to price gaps. This is why many investors only buy and sell overseas ETF shares during the hours when both markets are open.

- *Taxes.* Despite the fact that some ETFs have never distributed taxable capital gains to shareholders, the possibility exists. In particular, ETFs that track small- and mid-cap indices, such as the Russell 2000 and the S&P 400, can be less tax efficient than those mirroring a large-cap index such as the S&P 500. The reason: Indices of smaller companies are readjusted frequently as the firms move up the market capitalization scale. Whenever a stock gets dropped from an index—a small cap becomes a mid cap, say—the ETF must sell that stock, potentially generating a capital gains distribution to shareholders. Therefore, it's important to examine an ETF's distribution history as well as the frequency with which the index it tracks is readjusted.

Finally, keep in mind that some of the features of ETFs are better left alone, such as the ability to trade ETF shares throughout the day. This "benefit" may appeal to day traders, but it serves little

ETF RESOURCES

As ETFs' popularity has grown, so have the number of Web sites that cover them. Here's a short list of where you can go for general information about ETFs and details about specific funds.

- *The American Stock Exchange (www.amex.com).* The AMEX, which launched the first ETF (SPDRs) in 1993, offers expense ratios, investment returns, holdings, and other information for all 123 ETFs that trade on that exchange.
- *Morningstar (www.morningstar.com).* The Chicago-based fund-tracking firm now offers an ETF section on its Web site that includes analyst commentary, industry news, and a full range of performance and other data for the ETF universe.
- *U.S. Securities and Exchange Commission (www.sec.gov/ answers/etf.htm).* The SEC site provides a good general discussion of ETFs and their features, as well as advice on how to read an ETF prospectus.

purpose if you are trying to build an institutional-class long-term portfolio. Likewise, the ability to short sell an ETF—essentially a bet that its price will fall—can backfire easily and cost you dearly if your prediction about future price movements is wrong.

Instead, look to use ETFs intelligently—as an alternative to traditional index mutual funds when building a passively managed portfolio that offers unwavering allocation to the asset classes necessary to achieve long-term investment success.

NOTES

1. Investment Company Institute, (2003).
2. Morningstar, Inc., (2003).

Privately Managed Accounts: What's Old Is New Again

*O*ne of the more intriguing developments we've seen in recent years is the growing popularity of *privately managed accounts,* also known as *separate accounts* or *individually managed accounts.* These investments, new to many investors, actually have been offered by brokerage firms for several decades. But whereas privately managed accounts historically have been available only to the very wealthiest investors, they are being offered increasingly to those of us with more modest—albeit still significant—sums to invest.

Privately managed accounts are an extremely effective way to implement your plan if you're a high-net-worth investor with certain needs that can't be met by other types of investments. That said, they're not for everyone. We strongly believe that many investors, including those with large sums, can build winning investment plans using mutual funds, exchange-traded funds (ETFs), and other types of investments—an opinion that flies in the face of the many brokerage firms that are aggressively promoting private accounts to investors who simply do not need them. Because we are committed to the idea that your investment vehicle should never override your asset allocation strategy, this chapter will help you not only to understand the many benefits of private accounts but also to assess whether or not they're the most appropriate choice as you continue your journey toward long-term financial success.

HOW PRIVATELY MANAGED ACCOUNTS WORK

Privately managed accounts at first glance look a lot like mutual funds—both are portfolios of stocks, bonds, or other securities that are managed by professional money managers—until you get a look at their minimum investment requirements. Private accounts typically carry minimums of $100,000 or more just to get in the door, making them an option primarily if you've built considerable wealth.

In fact, wealthy investors are turning to private accounts in ever-increasing numbers. Assets in these accounts have grown from $161 billion in 1996 to $383 billion today.[1] This is still a far cry from the more than $6 trillion in mutual funds, of course, but it shows a definite trend on the part of some wealthy Americans to take advantage of the benefits offered by private accounts.

This trend is being driven by a variety of factors, including the fact that those $100,000 minimums were often $1 million or more just a few years ago. Despite privately managed accounts' recent rise in popularity, however, brokerage firms have been offering versions of these accounts to their richest clients for decades. They were introduced initially as an improvement over portfolios of stocks managed by the actual brokers at big Wall Street firms. Because the brokers were (and, we would argue, still are) notoriously poor stock pickers, the firms approached top money managers who served large institutions to manage money on behalf of their wealthy clients.

These days, investors are looking to privately managed accounts as alternatives to their mutual funds. But why would anyone consider an investment that looks like a mutual fund but requires that you pony up $100,000 per account? The reason is that private accounts come with a number of distinguishing features that bring a more sophisticated approach to investing that appeals to many affluent individuals, such as

- *Customization.* Investors in privately managed accounts can instruct the managers to avoid certain types of stocks or individual shares. Let's say that for personal or social reasons you wish to steer clear of so-called sin stocks in industries such as alcohol, tobacco, and gambling—think Altria (formerly Philip Morris), Seagrams, and Harrah's Entertainment. Your private account manager will identify any such shares in the portfolio and eliminate your position in them.

Also, investors with large positions in a single stock (such as company executives or founders) can ask their private account managers to avoid holding any shares of that stock. Thus a General Electric executive investing in a large-cap growth private account can avoid adding to his or her position in GE stock. By contrast, investors in mutual funds have no say over which stocks the manager owns. Index funds will hold stocks representing their respective indices, whereas actively managed funds' holdings are at the complete discretion of their managers.

- *Tax efficiency.* Investors in high tax brackets often favor private accounts for their tax benefits. When you invest in a private account, you own each of the individual securities in that account and therefore establish your own cost basis on each stock at the time you buy (in a mutual fund, by contrast, you own a share of the pooled assets and not the actual stocks in the portfolio).

The result is greater control over your taxes because you pay capital gains taxes only on the gains you realize while you own the stocks. Compare this with an investment in a mutual fund: When you buy into a fund, you also buy a piece of that fund's tax liability on stock that may have appreciated well before you came on board. If the fund sells that stock, you pay part of the tax bill that gets passed on to shareholders—even though you weren't invested in the fund during the stock's run-up in price.

Anyone who bought mutual fund shares in 2000 understands this predicament all too well: Investors that year were taxed on hundreds of billions of dollars in capital gains distributions, despite the fact that the typical stock fund lost money. That said, mutual funds' tax structure actually can work in your favor. For example, investors who bought fund shares in 2002 discovered that many of their funds were sitting on large capital losses due to the market downturn. Managers in these funds therefore were able to use those losses to offset future gains and reduce shareholders' tax bills.

Private account investors' greater degree of control also can generate opportunities to harvest losses in their portfolios, further minimizing taxes. For example, investors can direct their managers to sell poorly performing stocks and book capital losses that can be used to offset capital gains elsewhere in the portfolio or from an outside investment such as the sale of a business. With mutual funds, of course, individual shareholders have no say in which stocks get sold. This tax-management strategy has been further enhanced in recent years as more firms have introduced so-called overlay services that monitor and coordinate the buy and sell decisions of all the private managers used by an investor, thereby increasing the opportunity to maximize any tax-loss harvesting.

- *Transparency.* Investors in private accounts have complete knowledge of every security in their portfolios. Each account statement, for example, features a current, accurate list of all the stocks in that account. This knowledge of every holding enables investors to more easily understand how they're invested and determine if their manager engages in style drift. As a result, we tend to see less style drift in private accounts than in actively managed mutual funds, which disclose their individual holdings less frequently.

- *World-class management.* The best private accounts enable investors to gain access to some of the world's top investment firms. Many of these firms are virtually unknown to the investment public at large because they traditionally have managed assets only for large corporations and other organizations as well as extremely wealthy investors (see Exhibit 11-1 for examples of private account managers that we recommend from a variety of asset classes).

WHAT TO WATCH OUT FOR

At this point, the decision to choose a privately managed account over a mutual fund may seem like a no-brainer. Whereas a fund is akin to a bus, picking up anyone who wants to get on and dropping them all off at a series of predetermined destinations, a privately managed account is more like a taxicab or a limo that picks you up at the time and location of your choice—and drops you off exactly where you want to be.

The choice is hardly that cut and dry, however. If you're considering private accounts, you'll want to weigh their many positives with some potentially negative characteristics before jumping

EXHIBIT 11·1

Recommended private account managers (as of September 1, 2003).

Private Account Manager	Investment Focus	Web Address
U.S. Equity		
Ariel Capital Management, Inc.	Small/mid-cap value	www.arielmutualfunds.com
Atlanta Capital Management	Large-cap growth	www.atlcap.com
Brandes Investment Partners, LP	Large-cap value	www.brandes.com
TCW Investment Management Company	Large/mid-cap growth	www.tcw.com
International Equity		
Clay Finlay, Inc.	International core/growth	www.clayfinlay.com
Oppenheimer Capital	International core/value	www.opcap.com
Fixed Income		
Nuveen Investments	Municipal FI	www.nuveen.com
Weiss, Peck & Greer Investments	Core/municipal FI	www.wpginvest.com
PIMCO Advisors	Total-return FI	www.pimco.com
Specialty		
Lend Lease Rosen Real Estate Securities, LLC	Real estate securities	www.lendleaserei.com

Source: AssetMark Investment Services, Inc.

on board. As we stated earlier, private accounts are useful—but they're not for everyone.

Your first consideration should be the amount of assets you have to invest. In general, you'll need at least $100,000 to invest in a single private account. Obviously, you'll need considerably more money to build a well-diversified portfolio of private accounts that offers exposure to the full range of asset classes that constitute an optimal investment plan. Our experience tells us that private accounts are best suited for investors with at least $1 million in assets (a group consisting of some 2.2 million individuals in North America).[2] Investors with smaller sums typically can't build proper portfolios. Example: If you have $500,000, you can only invest in five asset classes. What's more, you'll be forced to weight all five asset categories equally. The problems associated with such inadequate diversification far outweigh the benefits that private accounts offer. In this case, a portfolio of low-minimum, tax-efficient mutual funds is a more appropriate option.

Investors also must consider their asset allocation and rebalancing strategies. Due to the transaction costs and administrative burdens associated with frequently selling a few shares of individual stock from each asset class and buying a few shares of another, private accounts are not ideal for investors looking to employ tactical asset allocation. That said, a more passive, or strategic, approach that requires periodic rebalancing is a strong fit with private accounts.

Also be aware that the customization feature of private accounts, while valuable to many investors, may not be as big an advantage to others. If you don't need to avoid particular securities due to your beliefs or due to a concentrated position in a particular stock, a customizable account probably won't really add any value. Think of it this way: If you've hired a world-class manager to run your money and you don't need to tweak your portfolio to reflect special circumstances, why not give your manager the freedom to do his or her job—pick winning investments?

Private account managers also typically review any customized requests before signing off on them. In most cases, a manager will do what the investor asks, but occasionally a request may be denied. For example, a growth manager may not honor a client's proposed restriction on technology stocks because doing so would conflict with that manager's investment philosophy and create style drift.

Another consideration: The managers you select to represent each asset class must be evaluated properly using a thorough due-diligence process. It is a foolish move simply to choose money managers from a brokerage firm's or an advisor's list of choices without first understanding how those managers were selected. We're seeing more firms cut corners by generating small lists of managers that they rarely check up on or fire if necessary. If you choose to perform your own due diligence on a manager, review our process for doing so outlined in Chapter 6. If you work with a broker or advisor, ask questions about the company's manager evaluation and monitoring process—and get answers in writing—before making your decision.

A dedicated portfolio strategist (see Chapter 5) can add real value when sizing up the managers who will be responsible for your hard-earned savings. The research capabilities and senior professionals found among portfolio strategists make them uniquely qualified to assess managers and track their moves for you. Once again, ask yourself, "Am I the most qualified person to make these decisions?" If so, you can begin your process of identifying specific managers. If not, we strongly encourage you to tap the resources of a portfolio strategist as you look for opportunities to make smarter, more successful decisions about your investments.

On balance, private accounts are not inherently superior to mutual funds, ETFs, or annuities—just as a fork is in no way superior to a knife or spoon. Each serves its own purpose and is a more useful tool in some situations than others. If you're in a position to take full advantage of the benefits of private accounts, we believe that you should look to do so. But don't ignore the other options that could meet your needs just as well, if not better, based on your own personal situation and goals.

The upshot: As an intelligent investor, it pays to keep your options open and not blindly buy into the hot product du jour. As we've mentioned before, some firms are aggressively pushing private accounts on investors who shouldn't be using them—selling a lineup of benefits that don't truly benefit anyone except the investment firm. We say this even though we offer private accounts through our firm because we understand that you're looking to make the right decisions about your money—and we emphatically believe in making the right choice over making the easy choice every time.

NOTES

1. Money Management Institute, (2003).
2. Cap Gemini Ernst and Young/Merrill Lynch, (2003).

CHAPTER

Hedging Your Bets Through Alternative Investments

*T*he extended market downturn that began in 2000 generated enormous losses for millions of investors and shocked many who falsely assumed that the lengthy bull market of the 1980s and 1990s would continue uninterrupted. In that environment, disillusioned investors increasingly began looking for alternatives to stocks, bonds, and funds that they hoped could help to protect their wealth from the financial markets' wild gyrations and generate profits when other types of investments went south. A growing number of those investors turned to *hedge funds*—a type of investment vehicle for high-net-worth individuals and institutional investors that first came into existence more than 50 years ago but has become increasingly popular lately with a broad spectrum of the investing public.

To see how the demand for hedge funds has grown, consider Exhibit 12-1. The number of hedge funds now stands at roughly 7500, up from around 2850 in 1992. Assets in those funds have soared some 441 percent during the past decade to $650 billion. More than one-quarter of affluent individuals (27.6 percent) invested in hedge funds in 2002, and nearly 30 percent anticipated using them in 2003.[1]

The question, of course, is: Should you join these investors in making hedge funds a part of your overall investment strategy? As you'll see, hedge funds are fundamentally different from most other investment options and offer several intriguing benefits as a result. However, hedge funds are also one of the most complex

EXHIBIT 12·1

Hedge fund growth.

Year	Total Hedge Fund Assets (billions)	Number of Hedge Funds
1992	$120	2848
1993	$172	3417
1994	$189	4100
1995	$217	4700
1996	$261	5100
1997	$295	5500
1998	$311	5830
1999	$480	6200
2000	$520	6500
2001	$600	7000
2002	$650	7500

Source: Van Hedge Fund Advisors International.

and misunderstood means of investing. In short, there's no easy way to decide if hedge funds are right for your particular situation. The best way to find out is to learn all you can about them and perhaps even consider working with a financial advisor to determine if hedge funds make sense.

WHAT ARE HEDGE FUNDS?

The question, "What are hedge funds?" can be a surprisingly difficult one to answer, because the term *hedge fund* is a sort of catch-all for a wide variety of investment styles employed by a diverse group of money managers. However, most hedge funds have one overarching goal in common: to reduce overall portfolio risk while generating a positive absolute return in all types of market environments. Hedge funds essentially attempt to do what you'd expect: hedge against market downturns. As you'll see later, the methods they use to do so are myriad.

Hedge funds pool investors' money and invest it in various securities and financial instruments. In this way they're similar to mutual funds. Unlike mutual funds and most other types of investments, however, hedge funds are structured as *private* investment vehicles—usually limited partnerships that can only allow up to 499 (and in some cases 99) sophisticated investors. As a result of

CHAPTER 12

their private structure, hedge funds currently do not have to register with the Securities and Exchange Commission (SEC) and therefore don't have to follow many of the reporting rules and other regulations that govern mutual funds. For example, most hedge funds won't send you detailed performance reports spelling out which securities the fund holds and the strategies used by the manager— even if you invest in the fund. In fact, gathering any specific information on a hedge fund can be a challenging job even for professional investors.

Because of the general lack of oversight on hedge funds, typically they've been available only to a select group of investors who meet strict criteria, which can include

- An investor who has earned at least $200,000 annually for the past 2 years and expects to do so again
- An investor who, with his or her spouse, has an income of at least $300,000 a year
- An investor with a net worth (excluding home and automobile) of at least $1 million
- An investor or a family company with at least $5 million in investments

Not surprisingly, then, minimum investments for hedge funds traditionally have ranged from around $500,000 to $10 million— making them the exclusive domain of the rich. Adding to hedge funds' snob appeal is the fact that, in many cases, access to a fund is possible only through an "introduction" by an existing investor or friend of the manager. As you'll see later, however, hedge funds lately have come down off their pedestals: Funds of hedge funds have now been launched with investment minimums of around $100,000.

To understand hedge funds' unique characteristics, see Exhibit 12-2, which compares hedge funds with mutual funds (we'll explore some of these differences in greater detail below).

WHAT DO HEDGE FUNDS INVEST IN?

The structure of hedge funds gives them the ability to invest in a wide variety of financial instruments to pursue their goal of reducing risk while generating positive returns consistently. Hedge fund managers take full advantage of this flexibility to invest in an array of highly complex and esoteric choices such as puts and calls and

EXHIBIT 12-2

Hedge funds versus mutual funds.

Hedge Funds	Mutual Funds
Private	SEC registered
Limited reporting	Annual reports required
Limited number of investors	Unlimited number of investors
Large minimums	Small minimums
Objective: Positive return	Objective: Outperform benchmark
Extensive use of leverage	Limited use of leverage
Extensive use of short selling	Limited use of short selling
May use derivatives	Derivatives generally not allowed
Cannot advertise	Allowed to advertise/market
Extremely flexible strategies	Relatively limited flexibility
Manager paid on performance	Manager paid on percent of assets managed

Source: AssetMark Investment Services, Inc.

options and futures, as well as more traditional investments such as stocks and bonds. They can make big bets on one area of the financial markets, engage in short selling (betting that the price of a stock or index will fall), focus on shares of distressed companies in financial trouble, and make aggressive use of leverage (borrowed money) to enhance returns.

Essentially, hedge fund managers have few limitations on the types of investments and strategies they can employ. In contrast, most professional money managers simply are not legally allowed to pursue many of the strategies—leverage, short selling, and others—that hedge fund managers use every day.

Perhaps the best way to understand how hedge fund managers operate is to examine some of the many investment styles found among the hedge fund universe. They include

- *Long/short.* This approach attempts to take advantage of perceived mispricings of specific securities by taking long positions in stocks the manager favors and short positions in stocks the manager believes will fall. At any given time the fund may have more long positions or more short positions.
- *Market neutral.* This strategy invests equally in long and short positions in the stock market (hence neutral) in an effort to minimize market risk. These funds' returns often are affected very little by the direction of the overall market.

- *Arbitrage.* This is a strategy based on the belief that two securities' prices eventually will converge. Convertible arbitrage funds, for example, may take a long position in a company's convertible bonds while simultaneously taking a short position in the underlying stock in an effort to avoid risk. As the prices of the two securities move closer together, the fund benefits from both movements.

- *Macro.* Macro hedge funds attempt to exploit changes in global economies and markets that result from shifts in interest rates, currency exchange rates, and commodity prices. These funds often make large bets on one sector or market, and use leverage aggressively to "juice" returns. As a result, they can be extremely volatile.

- *Special situations.* These funds focus on companies experiencing fundamental changes to their business structure, including mergers, leveraged buyouts, spin-offs, and hostile takeovers. The managers look for mispricings that may result from investors' misunderstanding of these changes and their effects on the companies.

THE PROS AND CONS OF HEDGE FUND INVESTING

There's a compelling reason why so many investors—including large companies and endowments—are attracted to hedge funds despite their high minimums, lack of regulation, and arcane investment methods. Hedge funds typically are not highly correlated with the markets or with each other (see Exhibit 12-3). Such low correlation (remember, a correlation of −1 means that the prices of two investments move in opposite directions) gives you the opportunity to achieve strong performance in both good and bad environments and improve the total performance of your portfolio. In Chapter 4 we explained the importance of combining asset classes with low correlations, and many hedge fund styles have shown the ability to zig when various financial markets zag. Consider that the return of the average hedge fund from April 2000 through July 2003 was 3.3 percent—a period during which the Standard & Poor's (S&P) 500 Index plummeted 37 percent.[2]

What's more, hedge funds typically attract an extremely select group of money managers who are among the most gifted and skilled investors throughout the world. Perhaps the best-known hedge fund manager is George Soros, who has earned billions by

EXHIBIT 12-3

Correlation among hedge fund strategies and market indices. *(Van Hedge Fund Advisors International.)*

	Spec. Situations	Short Selling	Market Neutral: Hedging	Arbitrage	Macro	S&P 500	MSCI World Equity	Leh. Bros. Aggregate Bond
Spec. Situations	1.00							
Short Selling	0.67	1.00						
Market Neutral: Hedging	0.62	0.53	1.00					
Arbitrage	0.61	0.35	0.31	1.00				
Macro	0.65	0.44	0.59	0.50	1.00			
S&P 500	0.63	0.77	0.40	0.40	0.45	1.00		
MSCI World Equity	0.63	0.70	0.34	0.32	0.47	0.89	1.00	
Leh. Bros. Aggregate Bond	0.10	0.17	0.11	0.02	0.07	0.03	0.05	1.00

betting on futures, currencies, and other instruments through his Quantum Funds. One big reason why Soros and his peers are motivated to set up hedge funds is because their compensation rests largely on their performance. Hedge fund managers typically take 20 to 25 percent of a fund's profits each year as an incentive-fee payment. Another reason is that hedge funds, thanks to their unregulated structure, enable managers to invest essentially without constraints and focus entirely on their very best ideas.

That said, hedge funds simply aren't right for many investors. When considering individual hedge funds, the decision to invest often comes down to economics. Even if you meet the legal requirements to invest in a hedge fund, you'll still need several millions of dollars in order to achieve adequate diversification among asset classes. But let's say that you are among those wealthy few with millions and millions to invest. You still need to think carefully about the negative characteristics of hedge funds before jumping in. They include

- *Little to no transparency.* Unlike with mutual funds, exchange-traded funds (ETFs), or private accounts, you typically won't know what your hedge fund holds at any given time. There's a good reason for this: Hedge fund managers often employ unique strategies that would fail to be effective if more investors knew how to exploit them. Nevertheless, this aura of secrecy—especially given the numerous corporate accounting scandals during recent years—is one big reason why many investors steer clear of hedge funds.

- *Illiquidity.* Hedge funds come with lockup periods of anywhere from a few months to several years, during which time investors cannot access their money.

- *High fees can mean big risks.* Hedge fund managers are paid primarily on performance. Most funds charge a 1 to 2 percent annual management fee plus 20 to 25 percent of profits. In one sense, this is positive. The managers' interests are aligned with your own. The downside is that as we've seen with executives and their stock options, such a strong emphasis on performance-based compensation can cause managers to take on excessive risk and make huge bets that, if unsuccessful, can lead to huge losses. Perhaps no better example exists than Long-Term Capital Management, the highly leveraged hedge fund that in 1998 made a series of mistaken bets in the bond market that caused the fund to implode—it lost a stunning $4.4 billion in just 6 weeks—and threw the world financial system into turmoil.

What's more, hedge fund managers' interests are not always quite as aligned as they want you to believe. Here's why: If a fund loses money during a year, it must recoup that loss before the manager can start sharing in any future profits. As a result, many managers who experience big losses choose to simply close their funds, return the money to investors, and start up new funds instead of trying to fight their way back. When this happens, you may need to find a new hedge fund or invest that money elsewhere.

- *A difficult due-diligence process.* As you know by now, we believe that it's of paramount importance to thoroughly evaluate a manager before you invest, using the proven process we detailed in Chapter 6. Unfortunately, this task can be extremely difficult for most investors trying to size up hedge fund management. Because these managers do not for the most part reveal the specific investments in their portfolios, holdings-based analysis becomes a futile endeavor. This, in turn, makes it tough to answer a crucial due-diligence question: Is the manager skilled or just lucky? Comparing one hedge fund manager with another is also extremely tricky because the wide variety of investment strategies taken by the managers makes apples-to-apples comparisons almost impossible. Essentially, investors cannot count on much information to make their decision on whether or not to invest with a particular hedge fund manager. The process largely comes down to reviewing the experience of the manager and deciding how much confidence you have in the friend, business partner, advisor, or other source who introduced you to the fund.

That said, investors interested in exploring hedge funds can find important details through some hedge fund research organizations that offer unbiased information such as manager databases and hedge fund indices (see Exhibit 12-4). While these firms still may not be able to answer every important question about a manager's methods and skill level, they stand to do a more thorough job than most individuals in this often-murky area of investing.

EXHIBIT 12·4

Three leading hedge fund research firms.

Firm	Web Address
Hedge World	www.hedgeworld.com
Hedge Fund Research, Inc.	www.hedgefundresearch.com
HedgeFund.net	www.hedgefund.net

FUNDS OF HEDGE FUNDS

The most effective method for most investors considering a hedge fund strategy is to incorporate a *fund of hedge funds* into a diversified portfolio. Funds of hedge funds are just what their name implies—funds that invest in a variety of hedge funds. Typically, these funds have much lower minimums than individual hedge funds—often around $100,000 or so. Most also incorporate around 10 different hedge fund strategies. These funds therefore enable investors with smaller sums to gain access to the world of hedge funds and achieve a high level of diversification among hedge fund styles and individual managers. In fact, many large investors such as pension plans and endowments favor funds of funds for their diversification benefits.

That said, some funds of funds are more diversified than others. You might find that one fund holds three hedge funds with macro strategies, two with market-neutral strategies, two that invest in special situations, and so on. This high degree of style diversity can help to reduce the overall risk in the fund. However, some funds of funds take a more concentrated approach by focusing entirely on various stock market styles or sectors. As a result, these types of funds will be more exposed to stock market risk. The upshot: You need to carefully examine each fund of fund's individual components and determine if the fund provides a level of diversification with which you're comfortable.

Although funds of hedge funds are appealing, we remain concerned about one factor—expenses. A fund-of-funds manager, who evaluates the hedge fund universe and decides which funds will be included in the portfolio, charges an additional layer of fees on top of those charged by the individual funds. Typically these fees amount to 1 to 1.5 percent of assets plus 8 to 10 percent of profits. These fees often seem excessive when combined with the expenses on the underlying funds. In order to justify them, the managers must deliver extremely strong performance year after year. The good news is that these fees most likely will begin falling as funds of funds' popularity increases. We've seen similar patterns occur as investors increased their use of other types of investment vehicles, such as mutual funds and separate accounts.

TREAD CAREFULLY

Hedge funds are truly one of the most intriguing investment vehicles in today's environment and likely will continue to attract interest from investors looking for innovative ways to structure their portfolios. Their benefits—especially the fact that many hedge funds have low correlations with the stock market and can reduce overall portfolio risk—should be considered by many investors.

As we've shown you, though, hedge funds play by their own unique set of rules—and those rules aren't always easy to understand. We urge you to use caution and tread carefully if you choose to explore the more than 7500 hedge funds and the more than 1200 funds of funds that exist. The tried-and-true advice that you should know your investment and its manager well before you buy goes double when it comes to hedge funds.

NOTES

1. Merrill Lynch Investment Managers/CEG Worldwide, (2002).
2. Van Hedge Fund Advisors International, (2003).

 **CHAPTER**

Putting It All Together

*C*ongratulations. You've now learned what it takes to become a smarter, better investor—and you're ready to build your own investment plan using the lessons and strategies that guide many of the world's most successful investors. Before you begin, however, take a moment to review the six steps that will empower you to achieve your financial dreams.

STEP 1: PERFORM FINANCIAL SELF-ANALYSIS

The discovery process that we outlined in Chapter 3 will enable you to design a plan for being successful "on purpose." Start by drawing up a financial roadmap of your current financial picture (where you are now), your goals (where you want to be), and the best path to take toward achieving all that is important to you (how you'll get there).

Remember to clarify your investment goals—college tuition, retirement, and so on—and your time horizon, keeping in mind that the longer you can let your investments work for you, the better your chances of success. Then see where you stand relative to those goals by evaluating your net worth, your amount of investable assets, how much of your income you can put toward those goals going forward, and your liquidity needs. You'll see how close you already are to meeting your goals—or how far away—and be ready to answer the question: "How will I close the gap between where I am today and where I want to be down the road?" Using the financial calculators or advanced investment software we detailed in Chapter 3, estimate the rate of return you need on your investments to achieve your goals. The higher the return needed, the more money you'll need to earmark to growth investments such as stocks and stock funds.

Also review the risks you'll encounter along the way, such as market risk and inflation risk. Focusing on risk is a crucial but often overlooked step. You now know that by aligning your plan with your tolerance for risk, you'll be able to maintain your strategy in both strong and weak markets and stay on track. Failing to do so can cause you to scrap your plan at exactly the wrong moments. So examine various periods when the markets suffered big losses and determine the amount of short-term losses you'd be willing to accept in pursuit of your long-term objectives without terminating your plan.

Finally, remember to put all the findings of your financial self-analysis down on paper in your Investment Policy Statement (IPS). This document, used regularly by large investment firms, will spell out your entire investment plan—from goals and needs to portfolio construction, manager selection, rebalancing, and reporting. Your IPS will serve as a constant reminder of your strategy and the smart decisions you've made in pursuit of your goals. As a result, you'll be more likely to stay on track and not let the emotions of the marketplace disrupt your long-term strategy.

STEP 2: BUILD AN EFFICIENT PORTFOLIO

We've shown you that for every level of risk there is an efficient portfolio that will provide you with the greatest potential return. As an investor looking to maximize your success, you should select only from those portfolios which fall along the efficient frontier.

Your job in building an efficient portfolio is to employ the advanced asset allocation techniques of modern portfolio theory pioneered by Harry Markowitz and used by the world's most successful investors:

- *Understand the risk and return characteristics of each asset class.* Review the historical returns for each asset class, including large- and small-cap U.S. stocks, fixed-income securities, international equities, and cash. For example, stocks have outperformed other asset classes by wide margins over time. Then scientifically measure the risk in each asset class by using standard deviation, which tells you how far from the mean (average) an investment's historical performance has been. You'll see, for example, that stock prices fluctuate more dramatically in the short term than other types of assets and carry a higher standard deviation. That said, stocks' volatility falls the longer you invest. No investor who has held large-cap stocks consistently for any 15-year period since 1926 has lost money.

- *Determine correlation.* One key to effective diversification using advanced asset allocation techniques is to combine asset classes that don't move in lockstep with each other. In this way, a decline in one asset or market segment will be offset by advances in another. You therefore should measure the correlation of each asset class relative to the others to identify those capable of adding diversification benefits when combined together in a portfolio. Long-term government bonds, for example, are not highly correlated with overseas stocks. When long-term bonds zig, foreign shares often zag. By combining asset classes with low correlations, you'll reduce your portfolio's overall volatility and earn more consistent returns each year. The result: You'll build more wealth over time.

- *Decide which asset classes to include in your portfolio.* The more asset classes you include when building an efficient portfolio, the more opportunities you'll have to enhance performance without taking on more risk. This means that you should consider multiple asset classes—such as shares of large and small firms in the U.S. and foreign markets, fixed-income securities, and cash. Also look to diversify among investment styles, such as value and growth, which often move independent of each other and further enhance diversification.

- *Use optimization to generate an efficient portfolio.* Optimization software will calculate the combinations of asset classes that constitute an efficient frontier. The process involves inputting the historical characteristics (return, risk, and correlation) of your chosen asset classes, as well as estimates about how each of those characteristics will develop and change going forward. You also must make assumptions about the capital markets' future performance and constraint decisions about the percentage that each asset class will represent in your portfolio. Optimization therefore involves both science and art, and requires superior capabilities and a disciplined process to do it right.

- *Use strategic asset allocation, tactical asset allocation, or both to develop your portfolio mix.* Strategic asset allocation sets ideal target mixes of asset classes and generally maintains those targets over long periods. Tactical asset allocation establishes permissible ranges for each of the asset classes and seeks to shift the target mix whenever there are market opportunities that potentially can boost overall returns or reduce overall risk. In simple terms, strategic allocation emphasizes consistency, whereas tactical allocation focuses on being opportunistic and taking advantage of changing market conditions.

STEP 3: BRING A PORTFOLIO STRATEGIST ON BOARD

We showed you in Chapter 5 that portfolio strategists—teams of analysts, academics, and other investment experts—are a key differentiator between good investors and great investors. We believe that you will significantly increase your chances of achieving your goals if you use a portfolio strategist.

Portfolio strategists take responsibility for three of the most important factors that will affect your portfolio's performance: selecting asset classes, determining and maintaining target-asset mixes, and selecting and monitoring investment managers. These strategists are highly qualified to handle such tasks because of their global research capabilities, focus on asset allocation, and teams of experienced investors and academics who make up their investment policy committees. These capabilities allow strategists to develop proven systems for investing rationally, not emotionally— enabling them to consistently buy low and sell high, for example. The result for investors who use strategists: less volatility, more consistent returns, and greater wealth over time.

You can serve as your own portfolio strategist if you feel that you have the time, training, and temperament for the job—or you may prefer to delegate the job to a professional. If you favor an outside strategist, review the criteria in Chapter 5 for selecting one that matches your own approach to investing. Consider such factors as

- Do you want a strategist that uses strategic allocation techniques or tactical techniques?

- Can you get all the capabilities you need from one strategist, or would you benefit from employing multiple strategists with a variety of approaches?
- Do you have special tax needs that require a strategist with a tax-sensitive approach to asset allocation and manager selection?
- Would you be best served by a strategist that focuses on global markets or one that is devoted to the domestic arena?

STEP 4: IMPLEMENT YOUR PLAN

The right types of investments and managers for your plan will depend on many factors specific to your own unique situation. When making your decision, keep in mind the following:

1. *Your investable resources.* How much money do you have to invest? The answer is important because you need to make sure that the investments you choose allow you to gain access to all the asset classes you need to build an efficient portfolio. If your investable assets total $1 million or less, we recommend that you consider no-load mutual funds or exchange-traded funds (ETFs), which generally offer the benefits of low minimums, low cost, and effective diversification. If you have greater sums to invest, you might consider privately managed accounts, which offer additional benefits such as customization, trading flexibility, and greater tax efficiency.

2. *Your investment approach: passive or active.* A passive investment approach is best if your goal is to match the performance of the overall market or a specific index. To implement this approach, we recommend index mutual funds and ETFs, which track a variety of market indices. If, however, you believe that it's possible to add value and outperform the market through active security selection, you'll want to consider actively managed mutual funds and other investments that emphasize and deemphasize certain asset classes and market segments based on the managers' outlook.

3. *The quality of the manager.* You need to assess the managers running your investments to ensure that they are capable of delivering strong performance and maintaining a

consistent investment style (not engage in style drift). Avoid the mistake of relying on star ratings and past performance data, especially over short periods, to size up a manager. Study upon study proves that these methods won't help you to identify managers who can help you succeed. Instead, use the process we detail in Chapter 6—which examines a firm's investment process and overall stability, the experience of the managers and analysts, and their understanding of risk when building portfolios, as well as "hard numbers" such as the information ratio to determine if a manager is skilled or just lucky.

STEP 5: REBALANCE REGULARLY

The markets are constantly changing, and you must adapt your portfolio accordingly. In Chapter 7 you learned the tremendous advantages of rebalancing: You reduce overall risk by consistently and methodically buying low and selling high, thereby helping you to keep your plan on track and enhancing your wealth by avoiding the pitfalls of investing with your emotions.

If you take a strategic approach to asset allocation, you or your portfolio strategist will want to rebalance your portfolio back to its intended target mix every quarter. For example, if your desired allocation is 60 percent stocks and 40 percent bonds and a bond market rally has bumped your fixed-income percentage to 45 percent, sell some bonds and invest the proceeds into stocks to regain the right balance.

If you favor a tactical asset allocation strategy, you or your strategist will keep a close eye on the financial markets and rebalance based on opportunities among various asset classes and market segments. If, for example, U.S. stocks appear overvalued, you might reduce your target equity allocation and increase your position in bonds (doing the opposite when stocks appear undervalued). Over the course of a full market cycle, your allocation should remain close to your intended target.

STEP 6: TRACK YOUR PROGRESS

Surprises are nice at birthday parties but not when it comes to your financial security. This is why every quarter you should take the time to revisit the goals and strategies you set out with at the beginning of your journey toward financial success and decide if you're still on track—or if any changes need to be made to reflect new developments. Regular progress reporting will help you to answer crucial questions about your plan, including

- Am I making progress toward the goals I set for myself during financial analysis and wrote down in my IPS?
- Is the amount of progress sufficient?
- Do I need to make alterations based on any important changes in my life or on performance-related issues from my investments and managers?

Use the four steps in reporting that you learned in Chapter 8:

1. *Note any changes to your personal or financial situation.* Write down major new developments during the past 3 months, as well as any that are rapidly approaching. Significant life changes—medical needs, a job loss, an inheritance— can alter your goals or financial status and shift your risk/return profile.

2. *Review your performance.* Create a composite index of the asset classes you hold, weighted in the same way that they're weighted in your own portfolio, to review and assess your performance accurately. Then evaluate that performance to determine if it's acceptable. To gauge your performance against your stated goals, compare your portfolio's rate of return over various periods with the desired return you calculated during your initial discovery process and wrote down in your IPS. Also compare the *expected* returns for your specific portfolio over short and long time periods with your *actual* returns. This will tell you if your returns are reasonable based on long-term market history.

3. *Account for your performance.* What factors contributed to your performance during the past 3 months? Was your portfolio heavily weighted to an asset class that posted extremely strong or extremely weak returns? This fact alone may explain why you underperformed or outperformed your goal. Next, evaluate the managers you've selected to run your money. How did each manager's performance compare with the returns of the appropriate index and peer group? If you find one who

has underperformed during a recent quarter, examine the manager's performance over longer periods to see if the weak results are a temporary slip-up or part of a larger pattern of underperformance.

4. *Make any necessary changes.* You generally should try to maintain your long-term plan by not getting caught up in the short-term market "noise." However, there are times when significant events require that changes be made. For example, as a child gets closer to attending college and you need to pay tuition bills, you'll probably want to shift some assets into investments such as bonds and cash that offer relative stability and liquidity. If you discover that a strategist or investment manager has delivered subpar returns over a period of 3 to 5 years, you should consider bringing a new one on board.

A PROVEN APPROACH

The six-step approach that you've learned has been proven time and time again to work. If you follow it, you will indeed maximize your chance for achieving the most important goals for you and your family. In the next chapter we'll review various types of market environments that you're likely to encounter on your path to investment success, and show you how to implement your plan in ways that will help to ensure your success in both good and bad times.

14

Strategies for a Changing Landscape

If the past few years have taught investors anything, it's that the path to investment success is full of pitfalls. As you invest toward your goals, there will be bumps and potholes along the way—and sometimes the road in front of you will get washed out. Between the market peak in 2000 and December 2002, more than a third of affluent investors lost 51 percent or more of the value of their portfolios. Another 39 percent lost up to 50 percent (see Exhibit 14-1).

These financial losses also have been accompanied by an overall loss in confidence due to accounting scandals and corporate malfeasance at companies such as Enron and WorldCom. The result: Investors have felt a great deal of pain in recent years and are at the point where they think the worst of the financial services industry. We recognize that many of you are confused and feel distrustful of just about any financial advice.

In the face of the financial markets' often-wild gyrations and occasional enormous declines, you still need to meet the goals and objectives that you've set out for yourself and your family. This task can seem exceedingly difficult, if not downright impossible, in an extraordinarily tough environment. Too often we see investors throw up their hands in frustration and assume that they can't be successful when a tough market takes hold.

We disagree, and emphatically believe that you *can* achieve success consistently during both good times and bad. Implementing the

EXHIBIT 14-1

Estimates of portfolio performance from the market peak in March 2000 to December 2002. *(Merrill Lynch Investment Managers. Analysis: CEG Worldwide.)*

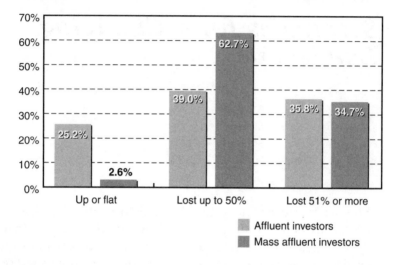

investment process we have described in this book certainly will position you better than the vast majority of investors out there. But even a proven, world-class plan can benefit from adjustments that reflect the market environment at any particular moment. In fact, you'll magnify your success if you adapt your approach to take advantage of the various forces at work during bull and bear markets.

Simply put, different markets demand different approaches. In this chapter we'll explore how you can align your strategy based on where the markets may be headed. We'll examine nearly 100 years of history to show you the long-term cycles that markets experience over time, paying particular attention to the type of market cycle that we consider to be the greatest risk you face in pursuit of your goals.

Based on your expectations for the future, you can use this knowledge to incorporate a variety of investment strategies into your plan and fully leverage the opportunities that exist in any market environment—be it bull or bear. Armed with these strategies, you will maximize your chances of staying on track year after year and enjoy a smoother ride toward your most important financial goals.

BULLS AND BEARS: SECULAR AND CYCLICAL

If we examine the markets over time, we see some interesting trends emerge. Historically, the stock market has experienced long periods—known as *secular markets*—during which prices move in a general direction. Exhibit 14-2 shows that the Dow Jones Industrial Average (DJIA) has gone through three secular bull markets and three secular bear markets since 1906, each of varying lengths and magnitude. As you can see, these secular markets can go on for some time: The 8-year bull market from 1922 to 1929 was followed by a 13-year bear market and then another bull market lasting an amazing 24 years. More recently, you can see the clear secular bull market that started in 1982—a period when Americans increasingly went from being savers to investors and benefited from such factors as falling inflation and interest rates that helped to create a truly enormous amount of wealth.

Take a closer look at what investors experienced during some of these secular market environments. During the 8 years leading up to the market crash of 1929, the Dow gained a whopping 25

EXHIBIT 14-2

Alternating secular bear and bull markets. *(Meeder Financial.)*

DOW JONES INDUSTRIAL AVERAGE 1900 - 2003

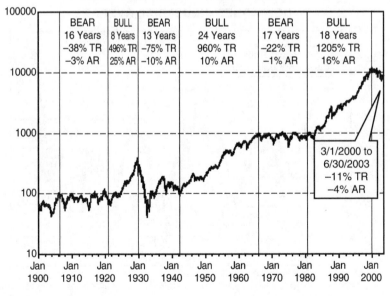

BEAR	BULL	BEAR	BULL	BEAR	BULL
16 Years	8 Years	13 Years	24 Years	17 Years	18 Years
−38% TR	496% TR	−75% TR	960% TR	−22% TR	1205% TR
−3% AR	25% AR	−10% AR	10% AR	−1% AR	16% AR

3/1/2000 to
6/30/2003
−11% TR
−4% AR

TR Cumulative total return over period
AR Annual return over period

percent annually; likewise, the index posted a 16 percent annualized return from 1982 through March 2000. For the most part, all you had to do during those secular bull markets was to show up for the game to earn big returns. Simply being invested in the DJIA stocks meant that you were a winner.

Now compare that to the secular bear market that started in the first quarter of 1966 and lasted until the third quarter of 1982. This secular bear took hold of the market for approximately 17 long years. Even with the recent market downturn, most investors today can't imagine a 17-year bear market. During that time, the annualized return for the Dow was *negative* 1.5 percent. What's more, inflation was extremely high, averaging 7 percent, making it a true challenge for investors to achieve a positive real rate of return from their portfolios. If you're like many investors we know, you'd assume that achieving success during a 17-year bear market is simply out of the question.

The good news: It's not impossible. Shorter market trends—known as *cyclical markets*—crop up repeatedly during long-term secular environments. These cyclical movements can mean big opportunities for investors during periods when the larger trend is negative. Consider our secular bear market example. Exhibit 14-3

EXHIBIT 14-3

Cyclical bulls during a secular bear. *(Meeder Financial.)*

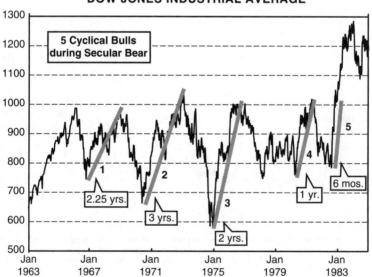

reveals that during that time there were no fewer than five *cyclical bull markets*—periods of strong gains from stocks. What's more, these cyclical bull markets remained in effect for anywhere from 6 months to 3 years.

The lesson of market history is clear: Investors did indeed have the opportunity to earn attractive returns during a 17-year period when the Dow remained essentially flat. The key, however, was to use the right strategies at the appropriate times.

WINNING STRATEGIES FOR BOTH ENVIRONMENTS

Now let's examine the best approach to take depending on whether investors are experiencing a secular bull or secular bear market.

In a *secular bull market*, success comes largely from being invested in the overall market. A passive portfolio management strategy such as indexing is an excellent way to invest because the market is essentially a rising tide that lifts all boats. You earn strong returns from the market itself. Active, fundamental research to identify superior individual securities and asset classes does not add considerable value to the portfolio management process in a secular bull environment. This is why index funds by and large trounced their actively managed peers during the 1990s and why investors have flocked to these types of funds. It's best, therefore, to own a broadly diversified portfolio that tracks the overall market, keeps portfolio turnover to a minimum, and maintains low annual expenses. From an asset allocation standpoint, you'll be best served by taking a classic buy-and-hold approach because in secular bull markets the key is to get on the horse, grab the reins, and ride as hard as you can.

In contrast, a *secular bear market* calls for a fundamentally different approach. During secular bears, active portfolio management is what enables you to achieve strong returns despite the difficult environment. The market is no longer lifting all boats higher, and identifying those assets capable of performing well becomes a much tougher task. Greater value therefore is added through fundamental research and the specific securities and asset classes that you (or your managers) buy and sell.

As a result, we tend to see a greater percentage of active managers outperforming a passive or indexed portfolio strategy. As an example, consider the period from 1965 through 1982. The DJIA began this period at 969 and finished at 1047—essentially the same place it started. Clearly, a passive strategy that sought to track the overall market would have produced disappointing returns.

However, when we look at how active management strategies performed during this secular bear market, we see tremendous success. The average actively managed fund gained 477 percent during the period—an annualized return of 10.2 percent (which, by the way, is the average return of large-cap stocks over the long term). If you had taken an active approach to portfolio management during this time, you would have bucked the market's negative trend and come out with hundreds of thousands more dollars than an investor who simply tracked both the Dow and the S&P 500 (see Exhibit 14-4).

Another key component of a secular bear strategy is to favor concentrated funds. You may remember from Chapter 9 that concentrated funds, unlike most funds, hold a small number of stocks—usually 50 or fewer—and that the top 10 holdings account for at least 30 percent of the funds' total assets. You also may

EXHIBIT 14-4

Benefits of active management in a secular bear market. ("Average Large-Cap Mutual Fund" represents the universe of 47 actively managed large-cap mutual funds with track records spanning from December 31, 1965 to December 31, 1982.) *(Brandes Investment Partners.)*

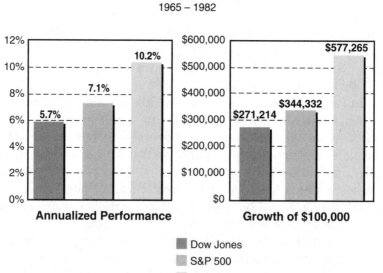

TOTAL RETURN
1965 – 1982

remember that concentrated funds have outperformed their non-concentrated peers in virtually all categories over time. These funds shine especially bright during bear markets because the value that is derived from active securities research gets "boiled down" into a portfolio of the managers' very best ideas. By having the freedom to focus on stocks or asset classes that are most capable of performing well in a tough environment and ignoring those with poor prospects, concentrated fund managers have a distinct advantage over indexers.

When making asset allocation and rebalancing decisions in a secular bear market, investors should incorporate tactical strategies instead of a relatively static strategic approach. The reason: As you've seen, cyclical bull markets often occur during secular bear markets—and the ability to take advantage of those periodic bull runs by actively shifting more assets into stocks can increase your returns significantly, getting you closer to your goals. What's more, various market segments manage to post strong results even in the face of a bear environment.

As an example, consider Exhibit 14-5, which shows the performance of several market indices and asset classes during the 1966–1982 bear market. Even though the Dow and S&P 500 delivered relatively unimpressive performances during this time, a few areas of the market—such as small-cap value and microcaps—

EXHIBIT 14-5

Annualized returns in a secular bear.

	Secular Bear, 1966–1982
Dow	−1.5%
S&P 500	6.0%
Microcap	12.2%
Small-cap value	14.8%
Small-cap growth	10.5%
Large-cap value	11.0%
Large-cap growth	5.1%
Long-term government bonds	2.5%
Long-term corporate bonds	2.9%
30-day Treasury bills	6.8%
Inflation index (CPI)	7.0%

Source: DJIA: Wilshire Associates; all others: Meeder Financial.

offered amazing opportunities, and easily outpaced other categories as well as inflation.

The question you must ask yourself on seeing these performance numbers is: "During an entrenched bear market, would I want to take a buy-and-hold, indexed approach, or would I prefer to have the flexibility to take full advantage of market opportunities as they arose?"

In Chapter 7 we showed you examples of tactical asset allocation strategists and how they benefited from their decisions to over- and underweight various asset classes to reflect market conditions. One of our investment partners, Meeder Financial, managed money during part of the 1966–1982 secular bear market with great success (see Exhibit 14-6). Notice the results of Meeder's tactical approach. On average, the firm delivered significantly stronger returns than the indices due to its opportunistic investment methodology.

We seek to be opportunistic in our own practice as well. In 2003, for example, we introduced a fixed-income hedge strategy to help safeguard against declines in the bond market, given our view that bonds had become overvalued following their big run-up during the preceding few years.

WHERE DO WE STAND?

No one can be entirely sure of where in the bull/bear cycle we are at today. Economists and market watchers are constantly debating

EXHIBIT 14-6

Meeder versus the market. (Performance results are dollar-weighted averages of private accounts managed by Meeder Asset Management, Inc., that have similar investment objectives. Results assume reinvestment of interest and dividend and capital gains distributions and are gross results before any management fees.)

Period	Meeder	Dow	S&P 500
4/1/74–12/31/74	9.5%	−24.0%	−24.4%
12/31/74–6/30/76	30.0%	73.6%	61.7%
6/30/76–12/31/77	21.3%	−10.7%	−2.3%
12/31/77–3/31/80	18.9%	8.2%	21.2%
3/31/80–6/30/81	44.4%	33.6%	36.9%
6/30/81–9/30/82	20.5%	−0.6%	−1.3%
Simple average of returns in each cycle	24.1%	13.4%	15.3%

Source: Meeder Asset Management, Inc.

whether stocks are about to soar, plummet, or trade sideways, and it's not our intention to predict the course of events over the next few months.

Instead, our goal is to help you understand the different types of markets that you'll experience as an investor and formulate superior strategies that will give you a fighting chance no matter what market conditions are like. If the bear market of the past few years does indeed turn out to be a temporary speed bump—a cyclical bear in an otherwise secular bull market—you will find that a passive, buy-and-hold strategy will continue to work well. Financial assets likely will deliver strong enough returns to enable you to attain your objectives by taking an indexed, strategic allocation approach.

That said, a secular bear market is the biggest threat to your continued success—especially if you simply maintain the type of indexed approach that worked so well during the 1980s and 1990s. As an investor looking to make the smartest possible decisions, it is clearly in your own best interest to face up to the possibility that the markets have entered into a long-term bear environment. Even if the bull market continues, however, there is no doubt that you eventually will be faced with an extended period when the markets move in a flat to downward direction. The roughly 100 years of market history that we've explored in this chapter proves that a bear cycle will reemerge someday.

How you respond to that market in terms of portfolio strategy and asset allocation decisions is what will distinguish you from the rest of the investing crowd. Instead of locking yourself into marketlike returns, look to enhance your portfolio's performance by incorporating the secular bear strategies—active management, portfolio concentration, and opportunistic rebalancing—that have helped the world's best investors achieve success time and time again.

For many of you, the recent environment also has caused you to reevaluate your ability to handle your own investment decisions. The power and freedom that some do-it-yourself investors felt by trading stocks online during the 1990s increasingly have been replaced by the desire for professional financial guidance and advice. Certainly, if we are entering an extended period of subpar returns from the financial markets, the right financial advisor can make a big difference on your bottom line by keeping you on track and looking for ways to make your portfolio work harder for you.

However, it can be a difficult job trying to identify those select advisors who can add value to the investment process from among the thousands of financial professionals out there. In the next chapter, therefore, we'll show you the benefits of working with an advisor—and offer strategies for selecting one who will truly serve you well as you pursue your most important goals.

15 CHAPTER

Selecting a Financial Advisor

As you set out to implement your investment plan, you'll need to decide if you want to handle all aspects of the investment process yourself or if you'd prefer to use a financial advisor. Recently, we've seen a significant increase in the number of individual investors looking for financial assistance and guidance from trusted professionals. In this chapter we'll help you to decide if it's in your best interest to use an advisor and, if so, how you can select one who will serve your best interests. There are an enormous number of financial services professionals out there who are willing to work with you—but there are very few who will implement the kind of approach we've shown you and help you to achieve the consistent long-term success you need to reach your most important financial goals.

After reading this chapter and the appendix that follows, you'll know the five characteristics that you should demand from a financial advisor. You'll also be armed with a list of the most important questions to ask that will help you to determine whether or not you should work with a particular advisor.

WHY WORK WITH A FINANCIAL ADVISOR?

The question, "Why do I need a financial advisor?" was one that many investors during the bull market of the 1990s asked themselves—and the answer was often, "I don't." As stocks soared, the misconception that the market was akin to a money-printing machine swept over much of the investing public. They assumed that earning huge returns from the market was as simple as being invested in it and executing $8 stock trades. Many investors in that environment couldn't imagine how a financial advisor was capable of adding any value.

However, after several years of dreadful returns and an enormous loss of wealth, investors are reevaluating the role of the financial advisor in building and maintaining a successful investment strategy. Nearly two-thirds of investors with investable assets of $100,000 to $1 million experienced as much as a 50 percent reduction in the value of their portfolios from early 2000 through 2002; meanwhile, 35 percent suffered losses of *more than* 50 percent. Investors during this time were reminded that investing is, in fact, not easy, nor is it a game that's fun to play in our spare time.

As a result of these astounding losses, we are seeing an unprecedented level of demand from individual investors for professional financial help. Exhibit 15-1 shows that 90 percent of high-net-worth investors are currently expressing interest in working with a financial professional, up from just 37 percent in 1997—not coincidentally, the year that Amazon.com went public and the tech stock craze revved up.

You need to ask yourself if you should join these investors in seeking professional financial guidance. Given the extreme ups and downs of the past few years, now is an especially good time to be introspective about your own investing habits, comfort, and skill level. Review your behavior during both the bull market of the

EXHIBIT 15-1

Strong demand for financial advice. *(Merrill Lynch Investment Managers; CEG Worldwide.)*

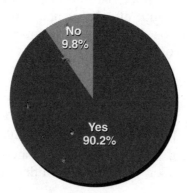

late 1990s and the most recent bear market. Write down honest, unflinching answers to the following questions:

- Did I invest in a disciplined and rational manner, for example, by consistently favoring undervalued asset classes while reducing my exposure to high-flying sectors? Or did my emotions—greed, fear, and panic—get the best of me and drive my portfolio decisions?
- How comfortable was I with my plan as stock prices fell further and further each quarter? Did I stick to a strategy that I developed based on my long-term objectives—or did I allow short-term market events to throw my plan off balance?
- Given the recent environment, do I feel that I am the person best qualified to make decisions about asset allocation, manager and investment selection, rebalancing, tactical strategies, and other crucial components of a successful investment plan?
- What is my outlook for the future? Do I expect another raging bull market that will require little more than a few index funds to achieve success? Or do I worry that a downturn could grip the market for many years going forward and lead to flat returns for the major indices—an environment that demands more sophisticated investment strategies?
- How much time and effort am I willing to commit toward constructing and maintaining the type of high-quality investment plan that will enable me to reach my most important financial goals?

THE BENEFITS OF FINANCIAL ADVISORS

If your answers indicate that you could use some help, a financial advisor can be an extremely powerful resource. Advisors offer several important benefits:

Benefit 1: Time. As you've seen, a successful investment plan requires a significant amount of effort and time. You must identify goals, determine risk/return parameters, draw up an Investment Policy Statement (IPS), design an efficient portfolio, select investment vehicles and managers, and perform ongoing monitoring, rebalancing, and reporting duties. Most investors simply don't have enough hours to devote to these tasks—and even if you do, you probably would rather spend your time with your family or on other activities. An advisor can handle much of the work involved in building and maintaining an investment program that works.

Benefit 2: Discipline. Behavioral finance tells us that emotions can be an overwhelming force when it comes to decisions about money. Scientific evidence proves that, as investors, we're predisposed to making poor financial choices at exactly the wrong times. By contrast, professional advisors who are devoted to serving their clients' best interests have the systems in place to consistently help you make objective, rational decisions about your money. An advisor, therefore, can help you make smart decisions during emotional market environments and keep you on track.

Benefit 3: Access. We've shown you that the select group of the world's best investors often does not serve the investing public at large. Instead, these investors focus on managing money for multi-billion-dollar companies, foundations, and other large organizations. However, an increasing number of these superior investment firms are now working with select advisors to serve individuals such as yourself. The right advisor therefore can provide access to the types of investment firms that can maximize your chances for success.

Benefit 4: Intelligence. Most investors simply do not have the level of skill that's needed to be truly effective. This is not to say that individual investors are incapable of achieving success. But the fact is that advanced training and market knowledge are key differentiators between investors who attain their goals and those who do not. The level of commitment required to gain this knowledge is beyond what most individuals are willing to make. Advisors, in contrast, devote themselves to years of learning about the markets and how to develop plans that take full advantage of how they work. What's more, most advisors are required to continue their education on a regular basis. As a result, advisors are able to recommend cutting-edge solutions that many individual investors could not come up with on their own.

NOT JUST ANY ADVISOR WILL DO

There are literally thousands of financial services professionals out there who are eager to count you among their clients. Unfortunately, a significant number of these professionals do not serve investors as well as they should. Many are more concerned about selling you products than they are about crafting comprehensive solutions that address the full spectrum of your needs. This means that you must do your homework to select only those advisors capable of developing an investment strategy that will truly help you to achieve the level of success that you desire and deserve.

The evidence we've seen shows just how important it is to find the right advisor. A mere 26.7 percent of investors surveyed say that they're highly satisfied with their current advisors (see Exhibit 15-2). The remaining three-quarters report the quality of their advisors as "fair" or "poor" and are actually willing to leave their advisors if they could find someone better.

The intense level of dissatisfaction among investors raises some important questions that you must ask yourself:

- *If you currently work with an advisor*, what is your opinion about the level of service and advice you receive? Are you highly satisfied—would you refer your closest friends or associates to your advisor, and would you readily give the advisor more of your assets to manage? Or are you among the vast majority who believe that better options exist?

- *If you do not currently work with an advisor*, you must ask yourself, "How can I find the type of advisor who will act

EXHIBIT 15-2

How satisfied are investors with their advisors? [Prince, Russ Alan and Brett Van Bortel, *The Millionaire's Advisor*™, Private Asset Management, Institutional Investor News, 2003, (New York).]

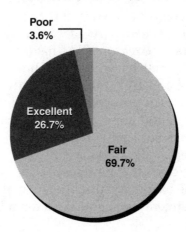

in my best interest at all times so that I can join the select group of investors who are highly satisfied?"

Keep in mind that you're counting on an advisor to help you to manage your entire financial future—and you're paying that advisor to do it right. As an investor looking to make the smartest possible decisions about your money, you owe it to yourself to be overwhelmingly happy with your choice.

FIVE QUALIFICATIONS YOU SHOULD DEMAND

In our more than 20 years in the financial services industry, we have worked both as advisors and with advisors. We know what it takes to be the type of advisor who can deliver what you need most: an investment plan that works.

As you begin your search for an advisor, there are five main criteria that you should use to evaluate all prospects. The select group of the very best advisors in the business will measure up well on all five factors.

Criterion 1: The Advisor Is a Registered Investment Advisor

Financial services professionals can carry a wide variety of designations and titles, such as certified financial planner (CFP), chartered financial analyst (CFA), and chartered financial consultant (ChFC). Beneath these titles, however, lies an important distinction in the way an advisor will deliver services to you—either as a broker/dealer (a stockbroker) or as a registered investment advisor (RIA).

We strongly encourage you to work only with professionals who are formally registered with the Securities and Exchange Commission (SEC) (or their particular state agency) as registered investment advisors. The reason: RIAs have a *legal fiduciary responsibility* to provide their clients with the highest possible standard of care. As a fiduciary, an RIA is required by law to always look out for your best interests and to completely and objectively disclose all important information in his or her dealings with you. By contrast, a stockbroker is not legally required to always work in your best interest. Instead, a stockbroker is held to a lesser standard of care that can create conflicts of interest.

Here's just one example: Stockbrokers may sell you a mutual fund or other investment that could earn them bonuses, vacations, or other benefits without disclosing that information to you. RIAs, however, are legally prevented from engaging in any situations that would serve their interests over those of their clients. This is what being a fiduciary is all about. RIAs also are required to provide you with a document, known as *Form ADV*, outlining the services they offer, how they are compensated, and any outside business relationships (you also can find this form yourself at *http://www.adviser-info.sec.gov/IAPD/Content/Search/iapd_OrgSearchInit.asp*). Form ADV is also where you can discover if the advisor has been sanctioned or disciplined by the SEC. Although few RIAs are penalized, this document will give you an additional level of assurance that the advisor is reputable and will work hard for you.

Criterion 2: The Advisor Uses a Fee-Based Compensation Structure

You'll pay a fee-based advisor a percentage of your portfolio's assets each year, often around 1.5 to 1.75 percent or so. As a result, a fee-based advisor's interests are aligned with your own: The advisor does well only if your portfolio does well. Therefore, a fee-based advisor is highly motivated to give you the best advice at all times. If the wisest course of action at a given moment is to sit tight and not make any changes to your portfolio, that's exactly what a good fee-based advisor will recommend.

Compare this approach with one used by other types of financial services professionals who earn commissions. A commission-based advisor may be more likely to suggest that you make a lot of transactions in your portfolio, even if they're not in your best interest. The reason, of course, is that the advisor gets paid based on the types of investments you buy and sell—and the frequency with which you trade them. Clearly, there is an inherent conflict of interest in this commission-based approach to portfolio management compared with a fee-based approach that does not rely on sales for compensation.

Criterion 3: The Advisor Is Consultative

Most advisors—even some who are fee-based—are trained to focus on specific products or investment vehicles rather than on a consultative service that addresses the full range of your financial needs. This is why it's imperative that your evaluation process weeds out advisors who are product pushers, leaving you with a list of advisors who employ a truly consultative process. This part of the evaluation may take more effort on your part—but it will pay off down the road as you develop a highly satisfied relationship with an advisor whom you trust wholeheartedly.

Advisors who are consultative work with their clients in fundamentally different ways than product-oriented advisors. Consultative advisors use a defined process for asking you a series of questions that uncover your goals and objectives, and use that knowledge to formulate a comprehensive solution. These advisors' goal is to develop deeper relationships with their clients that allow them to build and maintain superior investment plans. In short, they are focused on solving problems.

In contrast, product-focused advisors typically ask a small number of questions that serve mainly to frame their recommendation of the mutual funds, private accounts, or other products they want you to buy. Your larger financial goals and concerns play a small and sometimes nonexistent role in your discussions with a product-focused advisor. This level of commitment to serving your needs is not sufficient to ensure that you will develop a highly satisfied relationship with your advisor and implement a winning plan. Think about it: After product-focused advisors have sold you the product, what motivation do they have to continue to act in your best interest? As Exhibit 15-3 shows that subpar relationships are why most investors leave their advisors.

There are a few signs that will indicate if the advisors you are considering are product-oriented or consultative. You'll probably be able to figure it out during your initial meetings. Do the advisors spend most of the time talking about themselves and their firms' qualifications? Do they ask a couple of questions and then immediately recommend an appropriate product or two from among their offerings? If so, you're looking at product-driven advisors.

Initial meetings with consultative advisors are entirely different. Consultative advisors will ask you a series of high-level questions about your life, goals, values, objectives, and so on—trying to discover the "big picture." Instead of monopolizing the conversation and trying to impress you with their vast knowledge, they'll spend a lot more time actively listening to your responses to the questions and exchanging ideas with you. Perhaps most tellingly, consultative advisors won't attempt to sell you a specific product

EXHIBIT 15-3

Why do clients leave their advisors? [Prince, Russ Alan and Hannah Shaw Grove. *Advisor 2000: Strategies for Success in the New Millennium*, The Prudential Insurance Company of America, 1999, (New York).]

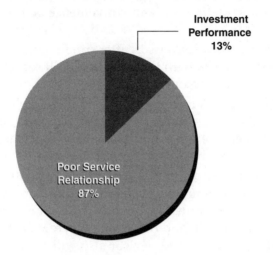

Investment
Performance
13%

Poor Service
Relationship
87%

right out of the gate. Instead, the conversation will focus on understanding your unique situation in as much detail as possible in order to craft a solution that factors in your entire range of needs. Only later will specific investments be discussed.

In addition, consultative advisors employ a formal, systematic process when meeting with their clients. When you meet with advisors, ask them to explain in detail the steps they go through—from the first meeting through the ongoing discussions. Here's an overview of what a consultative process should look like:

1. *Introductory meeting.* A consultative advisor will begin by introducing the investment process and the management team, and discuss the importance of a disciplined investment approach.

2. *Discovery session.* This meeting is designed to uncover your goals, objectives, financial resources, and time horizon, as well as return expectations and tolerance for risk. The advisor will use this information to craft a proposal that includes an IPS that chronicles your entire financial situation and makes specific recommendations.

3. *Investment proposal presentation.* You'll be presented with your personal IPS and investment plan recommendations

that show you how you'll get from where you are now to where you want to be in the future. Instead of asking you to move forward, however, the consultative advisor will request that you take the time needed to review the recommendations at your convenience before you commit.

4. *Implementation meeting.* If, after careful consideration, you choose to work with the advisor, you'll set up your plan and open the account.

5. *Initial review.* A few weeks after you've implemented your plan, you'll meet with the consultative advisor to review the strategy, review and organize the new paperwork that you have received, and discuss any other issues.

6. *Quarterly reviews.* Each quarter the consultative advisor will provide you with detailed performance reports such as those we profiled in Chapter 8. You'll revisit the goals you set out with and determine where you stand in relation to them. The advisor also will review any important developments with your investments or managers and recommend any necessary changes.

You can see clearly why we recommend that you work only with consultative advisors. When it comes to the management of your hard-earned savings, whom would you rather work with: a product salesperson or a comprehensive problem solver?

Criterion 4: The Advisor Incorporates Superior Capabilities at All Stages of the Process

At the start of this book we told you that good intentions are not enough to ensure your success. This message applies not just to individual investors but also to investment advisors. Often investors choose an advisor solely on the level of trust or comfort they feel with that advisor. These qualities are extremely important, but they overlook a crucial fact: Only advisors delivering institutional-quality capabilities—the ones found among the world's best investment firms—will be able to construct the type of plan that will maximize the chance of achieving your most important financial goals.

Your job, therefore, is to identify and work with only those advisors who deliver the highest level of skill and optimal resources at each stage of the investment process. Any advisor you seriously consider should use the type of six-step investment process that we've outlined in this book. By doing so, he or she will provide you with the same benefits enjoyed by huge corporations and endowments, including

- A comprehensive financial analysis (your goals, risk tolerance, return objectives, time horizon, and so on)
- An IPS that clarifies all elements of the investment plan he or she recommends
- An efficient portfolio representing multiple asset classes that will maximize your potential return for a given level of risk (This portfolio should be designed using modern portfolio theory and portfolio optimization techniques.)
- Access to both strategic and tactical asset allocation strategies in order to maximize your chances for success in both strong and weak market environments
- One or more professional portfolio strategists to evaluate and monitor all asset allocation decisions and investment managers as well as any special tax considerations
- Multiple investment vehicles—including mutual funds, exchange-traded funds (ETFs), and private accounts—tailored around your investable resources and preferred investment approach (passive or active)
- A disciplined system for regular portfolio rebalancing (strategic, tactical, or both) that will enable you to methodically and unemotionally "buy low and sell high"
- A thorough method of monitoring and evaluating your portfolio's performance on both an absolute and relative basis, your tax situation, and your progress toward your most important goals

Also note that the very best advisors in the industry recognize where they themselves deliver superior capabilities (managing relationships with clients) and where other types of professionals such as dedicated portfolio strategists can do a better job (asset allocation, rebalancing, manager selection, and monitoring). The advisor you chose should focus on doing what he or she does best and outsource other crucial components of the investment management process to more capable hands.

Criterion 5: The Advisor Is Someone with Whom You Feel Comfortable Working

You will be working closely with your advisor for many years or even decades—and your heirs eventually also may work with the advisor. What's more, you're counting on the advisor to serve as a partner in the investment process. Ask yourself: "Can I work with this person? Would I enjoy our meetings and other interactions? Do I get the feeling that this advisor will work in my best interest and help me reach my goals?" These issues are "softer" than many of the others, but they should not be overlooked.

WE WISH YOU SUCCESS

The information we've given you throughout this book will help you to become a more disciplined and successful investor. By seeking the expertise of a superior financial advisor, you will put yourself in an even better position to achieve your financial goals and dreams.

As you begin your journey down a more profitable investment path, we wish you all the success in the world. At the beginning of this book we invited those of you who were suspicious about the possibility of learning a better approach to investing to keep your "skeptic's hat" on. Now that you've seen how our six-step investment process can truly help you to better manage your portfolio's risk, enhance its returns, and achieve all your most important financial objectives, we think you'll agree that it's time to replace that skeptic's hat with a "smart investor's hat."

Our mission has always been to give investors the framework they need to make smart decisions, invest more confidently, focus on what's truly important while tuning out the noise, and realize their financial dreams. In the end, you owe it to yourself, your family, and the people closest to you to make the most of your hard-earned savings and live the life you desire. We encourage you to take action now. A better financial life is within your reach—if you make the decision to go for it.

Advisor Interview Questionnaire

On the following pages you'll see a list of the most important questions that you should ask each advisor you evaluate. Make copies of these questions and bring them with you each time you meet with a financial services professional—and write down what they say. Many of the advisors will give you answers that conflict with the information in this book. A select few will not. They are the advisors who can help to ensure your success now and during the years and decades to come. They are the advisors with whom you should work.

CONSULTATIVE APPROACH

- Describe your process for meeting with clients, from the initial conversation onward.
- How does each meeting serve my best interests?

DISCOVERY PROCESS

- What is your process for discovering and assessing my goals and objectives relative to my current positions?
- What methods do you use to determine the rate of return necessary for me to meet my goals?
- How do you evaluate my tolerance for risk in pursuit of those goals?
- Do you prepare Investment Policy Statements for clients? What type of information is included in the IPS? (Ask for a copy of a sample IPS.)

ASSET ALLOCATION

- Do you use modern portfolio theory to design efficient portfolios that provide the highest possible return for a given level of risk?
- What process do you use to manage risk in clients' portfolios?
- Do you offer both strategic and tactical asset allocation strategies?

PORTFOLIO DECISION MAKING

- Who makes the asset allocation and manager selection decisions for clients?

If it's in-house:

1. What are your qualifications in these areas?

2. What kind of team (analysts, researchers, and so on) at the firm helps to make these decisions?

3. What specific criteria do you use to evaluate money managers' capabilities?

4. How did you determine that you are the most capable person to make these decisions?

If portfolio strategists are used:

1. Who are your investment partners and portfolio strategists?

2. What specific tasks does each undertake in the investment process?

3. What investment methodologies do they use to make asset allocation decisions? Manager decisions?

4. How have they performed during bull and bear markets?

INVESTMENTS

- What types of investment vehicles do you offer to clients, and why?
- What do most of your clients invest in? Do you tend to favor one type of investment vehicle over another, and why/why not?

- How would you determine which investments are a good fit for my situation? What factors would you consider when recommending specific investment vehicles for my overall plan (amount available to invest; passive versus active; quality of investment managers)?
- Do you offer a range of portfolios with various levels of risk that I can choose from based on my risk tolerance?

REBALANCING AND MONITORING

- What is your rebalancing policy? How often do you typically rebalance portfolios? Do you employ both strategic and tactical rebalancing methods?
- Does your professional staff meet formally each quarter to review recent market events and how they affected clients' portfolios, as well as to assess if any changes need to be made? (If so, ask to review the notes from the last meeting.)

REPORTING

- Do your reports enable me to see how my portfolio performed relative to (1) major market indices, (2) a custom-designed index that matches up with my portfolio's asset allocation, (3) other major asset classes, (4) my investments' peer groups, and (5) my goals and objectives?
- What amount of real-time information, such as performance reporting and taxable gain/loss data, can I access through your Web site or other technology?

DESIGNATIONS/BUSINESS STRUCTURE

- What professional titles or designations do you hold?
- Are you a registered investment advisor?
- Do you have a copy of your Form ADV that you would share with me?
- Have you been penalized by the Securities and Exchange Commission or other regulatory organization?

COMPENSATION

- How are you paid for your services?
- Do you receive greater compensation for selling one type of investment over another or investments from one provider over another?
- How is your compensation structured to avoid any conflict of interests?

Index